The Harcourt Brace Casebook Series in Literature

Langston Hughes

A Collection of Poems

THE HARCOURT BRACE CASEBOOK SERIES IN LITERATURE
Series Editors: Laurie G. Kirszner and Stephen R. Mandell

DRAMA
Athol Fugard
"Master Harold" . . . *and the boys*

William Shakespeare
Hamlet

POETRY
Emily Dickinson
A Collection of Poems

Langston Hughes
A Collection of Poems

SHORT STORIES
Charlotte Perkins Gilman
"The Yellow Wallpaper"

John Updike
"A & P"

Eudora Welty
"A Worn Path"

The Harcourt Brace Casebook Series in Literature
Series Editors: Laurie G. Kirszner and Stephen R. Mandell

Langston Hughes

A Collection of Poems

Contributing Editor

James C. Hall
University of Illinois at Chicago

Harcourt Brace College Publishers

Fort Worth   Philadelphia   San Diego   New York   Orlando   Austin   San Antonio
Toronto   Montreal   London   Sydney   Tokyo

Publisher	Earl McPeek
Executive Editor	Michael Rosenberg
Acquisitions Editor	Julie McBurney
Developmental Editors	Laura Newhouse/Katie Frushour
Project Editor	Andrea Wright
Art Director	Vicki Whistler
Production Managers	Linda McMillan/James McDonald

ISBN: 0-15-505481-3
Library of Congress Catalog Card Number: 98-70271

Address for Editorial Correspondence: Harcourt Brace College Publishers, 301 Commerce Street, Suite 3700, Fort Worth, TX 76102.

Address for Orders: Harcourt Brace & Company, 6277 Sea Harbor Drive, Orlando, FL 32887-6777. 1-800-782-4479.

(Copyright Acknowledgments begin on page 153 and constitute a continuation of this copyright page.)

Web site address: www.hbcollege.com

Printed in the United States of America

8 9 0 1 2 3 4 5 6 7 066 9 8 7 6 5 4 3 2 1

ABOUT THE SERIES

The Harcourt Brace Casebook Series in Literature has its origins in our anthology *Literature: Reading, Reacting, Writing* (Third Edition, 1997), which in turn arose out of our many years of teaching college writing and literature courses. The primary purpose of each Casebook in the series is to offer students a convenient, self-contained reference tool that they can use to complete a research project for an introductory literature course.

In choosing subjects for the Casebooks, we draw on our own experience in the classroom, selecting works of poetry, fiction, and drama that students like to read, discuss, and write about and that teachers like to teach. Unlike other collections of literary criticism aimed at student audiences, The Harcourt Brace Casebook Series in Literature features short stories, groups of poems, or plays (rather than longer works, such as novels) because these are the genres most often taught in college-level Introduction to Literature courses. In selecting particular authors and titles, we focus on those most popular with students and those most accessible to them.

To facilitate student research—and to facilitate instructor supervision of that research—each Casebook contains all the resources students need to produce a documented research paper on a particular work of literature. Every Casebook in the series includes the following elements:

- A comprehensive **introduction** to the work, providing social, historical, and political background. This introduction helps students to understand the work and the author in the context of a particular time and place. In particular, the introduction enables students to appreciate customs, situations, and events that may have contributed to the author's choice of subject matter, emphasis, or style.

- A **headnote,** including birth and death dates of the author; details of the work's first publication and its subsequent publication history, if relevant; details about the author's life; a summary of the author's career; and a list of key published works, with dates of publication.

- The most widely accepted version of the **literary work,** along with the explanatory footnotes students will need to understand unfamiliar terms and concepts or references to people, places, or events.

- **Discussion questions** focusing on themes developed in the work. These questions, designed to stimulate critical thinking and discussion, can also serve as springboards for research projects.

- Several extended **research assignments** related to the literary work. Students may use these assignments exactly as they appear in the Casebook, or students or instructors may modify the assignments to suit their own needs or research interests.

- A diverse collection of traditional and nontraditional **secondary sources,** which may include scholarly articles, reviews, interviews, memoirs, newspaper articles, historical documents, and so on. This resource offers students access to sources they might not turn to on their own—for example, a popular song that inspired a short story, a story that was the original version of a play, a legal document that sheds light on a work's theme, or two different biographies of an author—thus encouraging students to look beyond the obvious or the familiar as they search for ideas. Students may use only these sources, or they may supplement them with sources listed in the Casebook's bibliography (see below).

- An annotated model **student research paper** drawing on several of the Casebook's secondary sources. This paper uses MLA parenthetical documentation and includes a Works Cited list conforming to MLA style.

- A comprehensive **bibliography** of print and electronic sources related to the work. This bibliography offers students an opportunity to move beyond the sources in the Casebook to other sources related to a particular research topic.

- A concise **guide to MLA documentation,** including information on what kinds of information require documentation (and what kinds do not); a full explanation of how to construct parenthetical references and how to place them in a paper; sample parenthetical reference formats for various kinds of sources used in papers about literature; a complete explanation of how to assemble a List of Works Cited, accompanied by sample works cited entries (including formats for documenting electronic sources); and guidelines for using explanatory notes (with examples).

By collecting all this essential information in one convenient place, each volume in The Harcourt Brace Casebook Series in Literature responds to the needs of both students and teachers. For students, the Casebooks offer convenience, referentiality, and portability that make the process of doing research easier. Thus, the Casebooks recognize what students already know: that Introduction to Literature is not their only class and that the literature research paper is not their only assignment. For instructors, the Casebooks offer a rare combination of flexibility and control in the classroom. For example, teachers may choose to assign one Casebook or more than one; thus, they have the option of having all students in a class write about the same work or having different groups of students, or individual students, write about different works. In addition, instructors may ask students to use only the secondary sources collected in the Casebook, thereby controlling students' use of (and acknowledgment of) sources more closely, or they may encourage students to seek both print and electronic sources beyond those included in the Casebook. By building convenience, structure, and flexibility into each volume, we have designed The Harcourt Brace Casebook Series in Literature to suit a wide variety of teaching styles and research interests. The Casebooks have made the research paper an easier project for us and a less stressful one for our students; we hope they will do the same for you.

Laurie G. Kirszner
Stephen R. Mandell
Series Editors

PREFACE

Langston Hughes: A Collection of Poems presents only a small selection of the seminal African-American poet's vast output. The works included here represent a sampling of the poetry he wrote at different stages of his career. These few examples, however, not only reveal changes in Americans' attitudes towards race over the course of half a century, but also offer readers the chance to observe a dramatic challenge to the dominant formal and thematic conventions of American poetry.

Hughes's poems present interesting problems for readers and critics, and the surface simplicity of his work masks vexing historical and interpretive questions. Why have the poems had such an enduring emotional impact upon readers? How effective was Hughes's challenge, through poetry, to racism and economic inequality? What was the exact nature of his relationship to African-American music? How should we understand and engage the "I" that speaks to us from so many of his poems? What should Hughes's status be within the canon of American and African-American poetry? Most important, we must be willing to explore the difficult history of American race relations. Hughes began writing poetry when social segregation was the norm in American culture. His poems challenged negative connotations of blackness. Despite the enormity of this task, Hughes was by no means narrowly focused, and his cultural and artistic influences were as diffuse as his motives. As an artist Hughes was driven by the desire to confront the social problems of his age and by the desire to become a better poet.

This Casebook will encourage you to explore the diversity of Hughes's work and the varied critical responses to it. Some of the secondary sources included here are meant to expand your understanding of Hughes's world and his commitments, while others consider Hughes's unique approach to poetry. All are meant to help you organize your thoughts, not to do your thinking for you. Nothing in this Casebook will eliminate the need to read the poems on their own terms; the questions, concerns, and pleasures you gain from the poems should dictate your writing and inquiry. A brief description of the sources follows.

- Hughes, Langston. "The Negro Artist and the Racial Mountain," "To Negro Writers," "My Adventures as a Social Poet," and "Langston Hughes Speaks." These four essays are reflections by Hughes on the role and function of the African-American poet. Written at different stages in his career, they offer glimpses of Hughes's encounters with the culture around him and show the ways that culture both encouraged and restricted him.

- Hughes, Langston. "Swinging High." This short story, which features Hughes's fictional character "Jesse B. Semple," illustrates Hughes's ability to address complex cultural problems in accessible language and forms. It also allows readers to compare Hughes's accomplishments in fiction to his accomplishments in poetry.

- Rampersad, Arnold. "The Origins of Poetry in Langston Hughes." Rampersad tackles the deceptively simple question, "How did Hughes become a poet?" He documents how a particular moment of emotional crisis for Hughes, a struggle with his father, occasioned a dramatic literary transformation.

- Tracy, Steven. "'Midnight Ruffles of Cat-Gut Lace': The Boogie Poems of Langston Hughes." Tracy considers Hughes's use of a specific African-American musical form—boogie-woogie piano—to challenge the impression that he was a "spontaneous" poet. The mastery of the musical form gives the poems, and the culture from which they emerge, a new cultural authority.

- Ford, Karen Jackson. "Do Right to Write Right: Langston Hughes's Aesthetics of Simplicity." In this essay, Ford evaluates Hughes's commitment to straightforward and accessible poetry, distinctly out of step with the dense allusion and fragmented diction that modernist writers saw as central to serious artistry. She highlights the necessity of such a method for a poet who meant to record the struggles of peoples living amidst racism and poverty.

- Beavers, Herman. "Dead Rocks and Sleeping Men: Aurality in the Aesthetic of Langston Hughes." Beavers describes how important the speaking voice and the willingness to listen are to Hughes's greatest artistic accomplishments. Beavers considers the "aural" aspects of "The

Negro Speaks of Rivers" and "The Weary Blues," among other Hughes creations.

- Hutchinson, George. "Langston Hughes and the 'Other' Whitman." Hutchinson investigates Hughes's relationship with the poetry of Walt Whitman, in the process expanding readers' understanding of both poets' accomplishments. The close ties between their poetries enriches our understanding of distinct African-American and American literary traditions.

Following the essays and story by Hughes and the critical articles is a sample student research paper illustrating the use of MLA documentation style and format. Student writer Grace Alston uses several sources to help her interpret Hughes's most famous poem, "The Negro Speaks of Rivers," and her essay is notable for the way she combines ideas from secondary sources, personal reflection, and careful attention to the poem itself.

Acknowledgments

No project as ambitious as the Casebook series happens without the help of many talented and dedicated people. First, I would like to thank everyone who was involved with the first and subsequent editions of *Literature: Reading, Reacting, Writing,* particularly Laurie Kirszner and Stephen Mandell. Next, I would like to thank the people who worked with me on the Langston Hughes Casebook: developmental editor Katie Frushour; production managers Linda McMillan and James McDonald; art director Vicki Whistler; and project editor Andrea Wright. I would also like to thank Michael Rosenberg, who suggested the idea of a Casebook series, and without whose enthusiastic help and support this series would never have come into being. Thanks, too, to acquisitions editor Julie McBurney, who is a welcome addition to the Casebook series. Finally, thanks to Kaine Osburn of the University of Illinois at Chicago who provided invaluable research support for this project.

CONTENTS

Introduction

Langston Hughes's
Twentieth Century

HISTORIANS AND CRITICS like to divide similar artistic responses within a given time frame into periods. Such a classification system helps them summarize the ways in which a particular group makes sense of the world aesthetically, and to evaluate how one artist is typical or atypical of any given historical period. Keep in mind, however, that these "periods" are simply convenient inventions, and that what we think of as the characteristics of a particular period—"The Harlem Renaissance," "The Jazz Age," "The Radical Thirties," and so on—should not determine our reaction to a given individual or text. This is especially important when we consider the life and work of Langston Hughes, who was productive for over forty years. At times, his life and poetry seem distinctly in step with those of his peers; at other times, readers must struggle with his individuality and distinctiveness. It is important for any student of Hughes to approach his poems with some basic knowledge of twentieth-century African-American literature and culture. Hughes was well aware of and sensitive to the unique conditions of African-American life, and he wrote a body of poetry that shows he was conversant with its turbulent history.

1900–1920: CULTURE AND ASSIMILATION

It is an understatement to say that the first decades of the twentieth century were difficult for African-Americans. Segregation was the law in much of the United States and was largely social custom elsewhere. In practice, there was little equality before the law, the vast majority of African-Americans were disenfranchised, and lynching was common. The dawning of twentieth-century American culture was darkened by the existence of virulent racism. Whether this racism was caused by white anxiety about blacks' social mobility (the recently freed slaves were perceived as an economic threat, competitors for scarce jobs and resources) or the tendency to identify and punish scapegoats at moments of social transition, a set of commonly held racist beliefs about African-Americans and African-American culture clearly existed. These beliefs—often antebellum justifications for slavery—were reinforced in the first decades of the twentieth century by both popular and academic culture. African-Americans were portrayed as lazy and inclined to criminal activity; black women were portrayed as morally suspect and black men as sexual predators. An early film epic, D.W. Griffith's *Birth of a Nation* (1915), was unequivocal in its depiction of African-American men as barely above the level of savagery. Minstrel shows, vaudeville acts, and other forms of theatrical production regularly used "blackface" and often parodied in music significant accomplishments by African-Americans. Popular novels, such as those by Thomas W. Dixon, portrayed African-Americans as unworthy of citizenship and expressed a longing for the reestablishment of the simple moral order of slavery, in which whiteness was unquestionably good and blackness was intimately connected to evil. Indeed, turn-of-the-century historians often described American slavery in terms that emphasized the beneficence of slaveholders and the suitability of Africans for hard labor.

Not surprisingly, middle-class African-Americans, the predominant African-American producers and consumers of literature, were cautious about asserting demands for change or celebrating the accomplishments of African-American culture. This African-American middle class had grown dramatically since emancipation, but the establishment and growth of African-American civil organizations, churches, and institutions of higher learning, in concert with significant gains in the professions (teaching, medicine, law, journalism, and so on), had led to the development of an unusual relationship between African-Americans and American culture. On the one hand, middle-class African-Americans could not help but recognize that in American culture as a whole they were considered pariahs. On the other hand, their success, even in the context of a segregated existence, led them to believe that if they continued to show their "worthiness" by emulating mainstream America's values, they would be rewarded in the long run. Much African-American literature of this era tried to reinforce this hopeful identification with mainstream—that is, white—American culture. Literary works expressed class aspirations and reinforced traditional American values such as hard work, thrift, religious conservatism, and respect for authority. Sometimes African-American literature of this period, whether wittingly or unwittingly, fortified ideas about the relationship between skin tone and intelligence or cultivation. For instance, heroism was most likely to be associated with light skin and a command of "standard" English speech.

Moreover, much of the poetry of this period studiously avoided racial themes and opted instead for the repetition of sentimental clichés. Most African-American writers and artists distanced themselves from the culture primarily associated with working-class blacks—the culture of blues, religious music, folklore, and vernacular speech.

Some African-American writers—Charles Chesnutt, Paul Laurence Dunbar, Alice Dunbar-Nelson, Ida Wells Barnett, and Pauline Hopkins, for instance—did make significant inroads against the overt racism and race anxieties of the age. But the dominant cultural and political tradition that Langston Hughes inherited (and, in many ways, set out to confront and change) was essentially conservative. Hughes's willingness to defy tradition—to make blackness his great theme and to take advantage of the great range of African-American creative themes and forms—assured him a place in literary history.

THE HARLEM RENAISSANCE

The First World War had a dramatic impact upon African-American sensibilities, in all aspects of culture. As would happen on many occasions during this century, war served as a catalyst for introspection. To what degree should African-Americans cast their lot with a nation that had refused to make blacks full citizens and partners? Should they answer its call to arms? On each such occasion, strong debate has surrounded these questions; on each occasion, African-Americans have served honorably and with valor. The First World War was especially important, however, as it served as a kind of community "coming of age." It marked the beginning of a dramatic reorganization of African-American life and also engendered an ongoing conversation about the real prospects for assimilation, a conversation that continues to this day.

At the same time, massive migration from the rural South to the more urban North (and to segregated housing in the urban centers), motivated in part by job opportunities in war-related industries, led to the establishment of large enclaves of African-Americans, communities able to support and encourage literary and other cultural activity. What is referred to as the "Harlem Renaissance" (c. 1923–32) was an impressive outpouring of novels, poetry, music, sculpture, and painting, along with the kinds of developments necessary to support those endeavors: artistic competitions, fellowships and prizes, debates about aesthetic standards, new presses and other means of production, advances in educational opportunities, and parties and other informal networking. Harlem—previously an Italian-American and Jewish neighborhood but by 1920 the largest enclave of African-Americans in New York City—became the focus of this "renaissance" (literally, "rebirth") largely because of the city's preeminence in cultural matters. Although cultural historians have appropriately considered this geographical center crucial to an understanding of twentieth-century African-American culture, it is important to keep in mind that similar outpourings took place in other urban centers, especially Washington, DC, Philadelphia, and Chicago.

The Harlem Renaissance is usually described in terms of the articulation of a new cultural confidence among blacks. The 1920s was to be the decade of the "New Negro." Putting aside somewhat the crude efforts at assimilation of the previous generation, this decade saw the emergence of a community willing to consider the beauty and nobility of an African past and to be more assertive in the articulation of its dreams and desires. There also emerged a willingness to challenge (or even parody) class sensibility and solidarity: one did not need to be middle-class in status or outlook in order to be respectable or successful. According to critics and historians who emphasize this new confidence—and who usually note the importance of African-American philosopher Alain Locke's anthology *The New Negro* (1927)—the most important legacy of the decade was the commitment of African-American artists and intellectuals to challenge standards of beauty in which "white is right." Partially motivated by the inevitable decay of African-American rural life signaled by the migration from the South to Northern cities, writers and artists celebrated, collected, and used African-American folk materials in their artwork. At the same time European modernist painters and sculptors such as Brancusi, Braque, and Picasso discovered African forms, African-American writers and artists began to investigate the meaning and importance of an African past.

Racist beliefs had sustained negative attitudes towards blackness in the previous period; now more progressive racial attitudes supported the growth of African-American intellectual activity. Particularly noteworthy were efforts by the anthropologist Franz Boas to overturn the crude hierarchy of races accepted by most nineteenth-century anthropologists. Boas challenged anthropology to reorganize itself into a discipline that no longer validated racist social policies. He asserted that all cultures were of equal value and that the task of the anthropologist was to document them before they disappeared. Although African-American writer Zora Neale Hurston perhaps benefited most from Boas's work—she was his student at Barnard College—all artists benefited from the way Boas's work stimulated interest in various cultural groups of the United States, including Native Americans and African-Americans. At the same time, continued interest in local and regional cultures and new conversations about America as a "trans-national" nation (an idea articulated by Randolph Bourne and stimulated by new waves of immigration) meant the efforts of African-American writers as diverse as Hughes, Alain Locke, and Claude McKay found a wide audience in important national magazines. This meant not only that black writers were increasingly coming to the attention of whites, but also that they were having an increasing say in a national process of self-definition.

Certain components of the Harlem Renaissance were controversial and still remain so. The financial contributions of white patrons and benefactors were part of the engine that drove cultural activity. Many of these patrons did not simply hand over money and step out of the picture. Some exercised tight control over the distribution of completed work and made the artists— Langston Hughes and Zora Neale Hurston, among others—feel dependent, like children with controlling parents. Other historians of the period have criticized the ways in which admiration of African-American culture too easily became romanticization. To some, "blackness" became a cure for the ills of modern life, an excuse for indulging "primitive" fantasies. For some whites, visiting black clubs or theaters, with little regard for the full-time inhabitants of the black community— "slumming," in the parlance of the day—was dangerous escapism. In other words, many of the negative connotations of blackness from the previous period—laziness, promiscuity, aggressiveness—were simply turned on their heads. Among some cultural elites, blackness became a positive characteristic, associated with simplicity, sensuality, and improvisation. Still, despite these significant drawbacks, the 1920s (as recent works by historians George Hutchinson and Ann Douglas have shown) was the decade that made permanent the intimate interrelations between black and white in American popular culture.

Focusing on cultural matters alone, however, limits our understanding of the turmoil of the 1920s. Sustained reflection on politics was also part of the Harlem Renaissance. While often criticized by the "New Negro" writers, the work of Marcus Garvey is nevertheless extremely significant. Garvey was the leader of the Universal Negro Improvement Association—a unique response to mainstream America's hostility toward blacks, especially the black poor. Garvey was a Jamaican immigrant who established a large grass-roots organization that sought to organize blacks as a self-sustaining "nation." For some, the establishment of a "nation" meant a return to Africa; others gave serious consideration to the establishment of a wholly black state within the United States or elsewhere in the Americas. For the average supporter of the UNIA, what was most important was the concept of economic self-determination. The UNIA organized churches and started businesses (including, most audaciously, a steamship line) largely on the nickel-and-dime contributions of working-class African-Americans. Charges of corruption led to Garvey's imprisonment and eventual exile from the United States; by the mid-1930s the UNIA had lost its mass following. The reasons for Garvey's downfall and the decline of the UNIA have been the subject of much historical debate, but there is no question that his dream of a black nation—founded on the belief that black is beautiful and not subject to the disdain of discriminatory institutions—had broad cultural appeal. The young writers of the 1920s—Hughes, Hurston, Wallace Thurman, and others—dismissed his nationalism as parochial and found his personal style crude, but they benefited from the change in cultural attitudes that he brought about. Not only did Garvey expand the potential audience for black cultural expression within the African-American community itself, but he also assisted in the more general assault on "whiteness" as the only measure of culture and civilization.

Perhaps more important than Garvey's contribution to this cultural expansion was the way in which he made obvious the decade's political dimension, illustrating that there was more to the Harlem Renaissance—or, more accurately, to the 1920s—than the establishment of a vital artistic tradition. African-Americans considered the possibilities inherent in the recent Russian revolution, and (partially as a result of W.E.B. DuBois's involvement in the Second International Pan-African Congress in 1919) they sought opportunities to organize across national boundaries for the improvement of the lot of black persons around the world. Without some acknowledgment of this internationalism and cosmopolitanism, one cannot appreciate or understand the events of the next decade, and especially the work and evolution of Langston Hughes.

Hughes thrived amidst the cultural and political turmoil of the Harlem Renaissance. He wrote stunning poems that celebrated the diversity of African-American life. He diligently drew attention to the beauty in everyday being and acknowledged the complex means by which individuals of all backgrounds and vocations used art, music, and language to give meaning to existence. It is difficult for contemporary readers to understand the uproar that surrounded the publication of many of his earliest poems. He was accused by black and white critics alike of peddling images of blacks that would diminish the community's image in the eyes of white America. He was accused of celebrating the "low life" and of not upholding art's commitment to the "finer things." However, Hughes survived this initial criticism and within a short time was universally accepted as black America's unofficial poet laureate.

THE 1930s AND ECONOMIC REALISM

If wealth and fantasy had much to do with giving the Harlem Renaissance its energy, it is not surprising that the onset of the Depression at least partially signaled its end. Economic downturns always hit marginalized communities the hardest. The Depression meant that funds directed toward the promotion of African-American culture became difficult to obtain; as a result, the writers and artists most associated with the Harlem Renaissance became widely dispersed as they, like many other Americans, searched for jobs to provide themselves with the most basic means of support. Moreover, the optimism associated with much Harlem Renaissance activity was hard to sustain in the face of staggering unemployment and poverty.

The depth of the Depression led many people—African-American artists and intellectuals among them—to consider the possibility of radically transforming the economic and political system under which it occurred. For this reason, many African-American writers—indeed, many American writers generally—were drawn to the Communist Party or to other political organizations in the Marxist–Leninist tradition. The Communist Party had achieved significant publicity and won sympathy among African-Americans for its support of the Scottsboro boys, a group of young African-American men falsely accused of rape in Scottsboro, Alabama. It was also one of the few organizations that provided explicitly interracial opportunities to organize for progressive social change. For writers and critics in particular, this relationship with the radical Left meant that much of the 1930s was spent attempting to articulate what the relationship between writing and social transformation might be. Dynamic (and sometimes not so dynamic) new forms of poetry, fiction, and drama emerged from this complex conversation.

Not surprisingly, perhaps, it is not the more directly confrontational works of African-American writers of the 1930s, but rather works of racial affirmation from the 1920s—say, Hughes's "The Negro Speaks of Rivers" or Jean Toomer's *Cane*—that are the most widely anthologized works of African-American literature. In a culture that still too easily and too often expresses its contempt for black cultural expression, this should be cause for celebration. But the best of the work of the 1930s—including the fiction of William Attaway, the poetry of Frank Marshall Davis, and the poetry of

Hughes himself—deserves more attention. Other writers of the 1930s, most notably Arna Bontemps and Sterling Brown, carried the predominant concerns of the 1920s into the 1930s, and their work too is worthy of further attention. By focusing unromantically on the accomplishments and limitations of largely Southern and rural black folk and the landscape they inhabited, these writers discovered that the articulation of black pride and a critique of the prevailing economic order were not mutually exclusive. Hughes too understood this, and his poetry of the 1930s and 1940s—while distinct from that of Bontemps and Brown—reflected this insight.

The rise of fascism on the international scene in the middle of the 1930s, especially in Spain, Germany, and Italy, was also a source of significant consciousness-raising among African-American writers. The assault on Republican Spain, the racist philosophies of Adolph Hitler, and Mussolini's attack on Ethiopia led to the continued internationalization of African-American writing and to black participation in a variety of protests. Toward the end of the decade, and not without controversy, some of the incisive economic demands of the radical Left were put aside as Americans put up a "popular front" against the fascist threat. Hughes was at the center of these developments, too. He traveled to Spain and wrote moving poetry and essays that celebrated the international (and interracial) effort to save the Republic, and later offered works that elegized its fall. Despite the single-minded opposition to these international threats—in particular, the threat of Hitler—Hughes's poetry continued to explore the interrelated themes of fascism, racism, and economic inequality on the domestic and international scenes.

THE 1940s AND 1950s: THE POETICS
OF INTEGRATION AND DISINTEGRATION

This period of African-American cultural history is among the most difficult to summarize. On the one hand, the defeat of fascism in the Second World War led to a kind of optimism not unlike that which followed the First World War. On the other hand, the experience of African-Americans during the war was ambivalent at best. Continued segregation in combat units, frustration in gaining equal employment opportunities in war industries, and continued experience with segregated public facilities led to significant cultural conflicts. Civil disturbances in Harlem and Detroit and deadly interracial conflicts at a number of U.S. military bases suggested the turmoil that lay beneath the surface.

During the postwar period, a group of writers and artists based largely in Chicago, Richard Wright and Margaret Walker most notable among them, attempted to sustain the energies that had promoted literary activity in the 1920s and 1930s. Like Brown and Bontemps, this group of writers did not see the distinction between affirming blackness and critiquing the culture at large. Although not associated with the "Chicago school," Chester Himes and Ann Petry also wrote important novels that continued to question American culture. To varying degrees, all of these writers sought to contend with the continued transformation of African-American life, while during these years another great migration occurred, again moving tens of thousands of African-Americans from South to North. Most important, they meant to comment on the process by which black "enclaves" became impoverished, isolated ghettoes. All the while, these writers attempted to make audiences more comfortable with the great variety of black cultural expression. Even poets Robert Hayden, Gwendolyn Brooks, and Melvin Tolson, all students of literary modernism and ostensibly academic in orientation, continued to imagine new ways in which their literary expression could simultaneously be beautiful and serve as a vehicle of change.

By the 1950s, however, this confidence had begun to erode. Some writers came to believe that the horrors of the Second World War and related events—the Holocaust, the dropping of the atomic bomb, increasing knowledge of the purges in Russia, continued racism and inequality at home—made necessary the production of a literature that was explicitly or implicitly more skeptical of attempts to change the world. Increasingly, writers tried to distance themselves from politics. Their work grew more philosophic and meditative and, on occasion, more self-consciously experimental and interracial. The poetry of Owen Dodson and the novels of William Demby, James Baldwin, and Ralph Ellison are typical of this period. Of course, this is not to say that these writers were unconcerned about racism or that they were unwilling to confront American culture directly. In fact, many of the writers who were most critical of "politics" were those most alienated from the status quo. Many of these writers, some aided by the G.I. Bill, left the United States temporarily or permanently in order to discover a new perspective on their work and homeland. To many, expatriation seemed an appropriate response to a culture increasingly unclear about its central values. The United States was still largely hypocritical in its treatment of its black citizens; it was increasingly an advocate of freedom abroad, but a large portion of its own population was without basic human rights.

To understand this subtle shift in black writing from direct confrontation and "hard" realism to indirect critique and celebration of irony and ambiguity, it is important to note the influence of the onset of the Cold War. The articulation of incisive, direct, and blunt criticism of American culture became increasingly difficult. The establishment of the House Un-American Activities Committee, and the blacklisting of thinkers from a number of cultural institutions, including universities, made individuals of all races afraid to challenge the injustices of American society. Many American writers were forced to publicly reassess, if not renounce, their past political commitments. Hughes found himself in this difficult situation, meditating publicly about the costs and accomplishments of his "social poetry." (Hughes chose not to include many of these poems in his 1959 *Selected Poems*.) Other African-American writers, however, continued to articulate the circumstances of black people in terms of race and class politics. W.E.B. DuBois, John O. Killens, Lorraine Hansberry, Lloyd Brown, Ray Durem, and others wrote fiction, poetry, and drama that explored the possibilities of an explicitly ideological art. Another strategy was pursued by African-American poets like Bob Kaufman, Ted Joans, and a young Leroi Jones (later known as Amiri Baraka), who participated in artistic movements that defined their reason for being largely in aesthetic terms but often contained substantive critiques of American culture.

Ironically, it is possible to argue that the culture of the Cold War, despite its repressive atmosphere, helped advance the Civil Rights movement, eventually leading to the next great outpouring of African-American artistry. Because the United States was involved in a global debate about the superiority of the American way of life, it could not afford to be seen as a racist nation. Some historians have recently argued that sensitivity to the United States' image abroad led to the emergence of a loose commitment on the part of American leaders to challenge the legal and social basis for segregation. This openness—and, more significantly, the heroic actions of tens of thousands of African-Americans and their white allies who participated in nonviolent civil disobedience—eventually led to changes in American race relations. The process of decolonization also had a positive impact on African-American writers. As the 1950s came to a close, the slow process— itself a byproduct of Cold War geopolitics—by which the main imperial powers, Great Britain and France, granted political independence to their mostly black overseas colonies, produced concrete results. In 1957, independence was granted to the Gold Coast, which changed its name to Ghana— a development that was received enthusiastically among African-American creative intellectuals. Decolonization became connected with the Civil Rights movement, creating a new cultural optimism that served as a foundation for the next renaissance of black artistry.

How does Langston Hughes fit into this complex picture? His late 1940s and 1950s poetry is more self-consciously invested in experiments with poetic form than his earlier work, yet he never abandoned his social and political aims. And while Hughes, more than any other African-American writer with the exception of W.E.B. DuBois, was severely scarred by the 1950s anti-Communist witch hunts, the Civil Rights movement and decolonization affirmed his confidence in the unity of black folk and his hopes for a possible coalition of black people around the world. These positive influences encouraged, perhaps even made possible, his most ambitious book of poetry, *Ask Your Mama* (1961).

THE 1960s AND THE BLACK ARTS MOVEMENT

The optimism associated with liberation movements both at home and abroad had a distinct influence on the literature of the 1960s. Although some African-American literature described recurrent race violence with pessimism, the decade eventually became known for its frank consideration of the possibility of a "black aesthetic." Pursuit of social and political liberation initiated some striking reflection in the area of culture, too. If black people around the world could reject servitude to their white political masters, could similar assaults be made upon aesthetic and cultural hierarchies as well? The most straightforward formulation of this idea was the Black Arts movement: "black art for black people according to black standards of criticism." Black Arts adherents celebrated urban African-American speech as crucial to the development of a unique black artistry. They encouraged the systematic consideration of black beauty, heroes, and mythologies and insisted that black art not be subjected to Eurocentric critical standards. (More so than fiction, poetry was the product of this vanguard artistry. Because poetry could be produced and distributed cheaply, it more easily challenged convention.) They also had a specific interest in the development of black-owned and directed publishing houses, magazines and journals, and they encouraged the establishment of African-American Studies programs at colleges and universities. The movement led to the emergence of a number of well-regarded literary artists, such as Amiri Baraka, a.b. spellman, and Sonia Sanchez and critics, such as Larry Neal and Hoyt Fuller, and the establishment of seminal cultural institutions, such as Broadside Press, Third World Press, and *Black Scholar* magazine. The breadth and energy of these developments have led some commentators to refer to the period (c. 1960–72) as the "Second Black Renaissance."

The "New Black Poetry" can be seen as an extension (and, sometimes, as an exaggeration) of much of what had come before. Although the new poets of the 1960s tended to emphasize their break with the past, they were in many ways repeating the generational shift that Hughes and his peers in the 1920s had first undertaken. As in the Harlem Renaissance, a group of younger artists and intellectuals criticized forces within and outside the African-American community who supported an uncritical assimilationism. What may be distinct about the Black Arts poets is the breadth and urgency of their cultural criticism. The chaos of much of American life in the 1960s—the Vietnam War, the assassinations of Malcolm X, Medgar Evers, Martin Luther King, Jr., and John and Robert Kennedy, the urban rebellions—made this a necessity.

Many of those in the new generation of poets were unclear about what to make of the accomplishments of their forebears, and Hughes himself came under their close scrutiny. While certainly respected, his work seemed passé to some. Hughes's commitment to black pride was unmistakable, but the racial rhetoric and treatment of black urban culture in his work seemed much too restrained. Ironically, Hughes had gone from being perceived as a racial iconoclast in the 1920s and a political radical in the 1930s to being seen in his last decade as a somewhat timid figure, however readable and accomplished. In many ways, the hesitancy among younger black poets to claim Hughes as a model was unfortunate. Hughes's portrayal of women, for instance, while by no means feminist, displayed a degree of subtlety missing in much Black Arts poetry. And Hughes might have taught the Black Arts poets a great deal about the relationship between politics and culture, poetry and calls for revolution. His posthumous work, *The Panther and the Lash* (1967), evoking for some the emergence of the Black Power movement, demonstrated that he had by no means become an anachronism. If not always directly confrontational, the poems in this collection were as topical and relevant as those of the most well-known younger poets: Amiri Baraka, Nikki Giovanni, Etheridge Knight, Don L. Lee, or Sonia Sanchez. It is clear that Hughes was not so much out of step with the demands of this turbulent decade as he was chastened by his experience of the previous four.

LANGSTON HUGHES AND THE LIMITS
OF AFRICAN-AMERICAN CULTURAL HISTORY

The preceding discussion emphasizes the development of literary and cultural consciousness among African-Americans over and against the complexities of American race relations. It provides some means to understand Hughes's accomplishments as a poet in the United States over the course of his career and the cultural impact he has had in this country. Other cultural contexts, of course, generate other insights and knowledge.

For instance, one of the limitations of placing Hughes within a distinctly literary context is that he, like many other African-American poets and novelists, took his primary artistic cues from, and often hoped to be judged alongside, musicians. An alternative introduction to Hughes's work might view the imperatives of musical performance—improvisatory skill and distinctive voice—as the most important means by which we make sense of his accomplishments. Such an essay might highlight the ways in which black music has been an important cross-cultural meeting ground in American life, and, as such, important in the creation of individual and collective identity. This cultural context might reveal in Hughes's poetry the manifold ways in which black and white Americans use each other as a kind of mirror with which to evaluate their progress, or his attempt to capture joy and pleasure, popular music's appeal to the body, in verse.

It is also worth noting that a credible context can be constructed for viewing Hughes's work in terms of ideas and movements that developed outside the United States. Hughes maintained friendships with or was connected to a who's who of the international literary scene: Aimé Cesaire of Martinique, Nicolás Guillén of Cuba, Federico García Lorca of Spain, Jacques Roumain of Haiti, Leopold Senghor of Senegal, and many others. An alternative background essay might highlight cultural developments among the diaspora of black peoples around the world, or it might consider Hughes's role as a cultural mediator. This last approach might reveal in Hughes's poetry a legacy of cross-cultural connections and political ambitions and an impressive attempt on the part of one individual to come to terms with the twentieth century's most dramatic social and political transformations.

For the student of Hughes's poetry, then, the task is to take full account of the social context in which Hughes wrote, yet—perceiving the great diversity of responses to that social context and the numerous ways in which that context can be constructed—always take seriously the individuality of the poem itself.

WORKS CONSULTED

Bell, Bernard. *The Afro-American Novel and Its Tradition.* Amherst: U of Massachusetts P, 1987.

Douglas, Ann. *Terrible Honesty: Mongrel Manhattan in the 1920s.* New York: Farrer, 1995.

Hutchinson, George. *The Harlem Renaissance in Black and White.* Cambridge, MA: Harvard UP, 1995.

Johnson, Abby Arthur, and Ronald Maberry Johnson. *Propaganda and Aesthetics: The Literary Politics of African-American Magazines in the Twentieth Century.* Amherst: U of Massachusetts P, 1991.

Lewis, David Levering. *When Harlem Was In Vogue.* New York: Knopf, 1981.

Miller, James. "African-American Writing of the 1930s: A Prologue." In *Radical Revisions: Rereading 1930s Culture.* Ed. Bill Mullen and Sherry Lee Linkon. Urbana: U of Illinois P, 1996.

Smith, David Lionel. "The Black Arts Movement and Its Critics." *American Literary History* 3.1 (1991): 93–110.

Wald, Alan. *Writing From the Left: New Essays on Radical Culture and Politics.* New York: Verso, 1994.

About the Author

LANGSTON HUGHES (1902–67) is often referred to as the most accomplished African-American poet of the twentieth century. He was also a skilled fiction writer, playwright, autobiographer, and essayist. Although most people associate him with the Harlem Renaissance, he was a cosmopolitan man, a world traveler who wrote significant works of imaginative literature for close to half a century. Nevertheless, more than anything else his poetry gives evidence to his great love for African-American people and their culture.

Born in Joplin, Missouri, he was reared throughout the Midwest. His formal education included time spent at Columbia University and the historically black Lincoln University, from which he graduated in 1929. Perhaps more important than his formal education, however, were the years he spent working on a ship traveling to Europe and Africa, and his visits to Mexico to see his father, a successful entrepreneur but indifferent parent. His artwork, especially his monumental first books *The Weary Blues* (1926) and *Fine Clothes for the Jew* (1927), eventually provided the opportunity for further travel, to the Soviet Union, to Europe on the eve of the Second World War, and, late in life, once again to Africa. Significantly, he wrote his earliest poems while working as a busboy and performing other common labor. His informal education—acquired through travel and hard work—consolidated his appreciation for common folk throughout the world, their day-to-day struggles, and the often beautiful art they produced as a means of ordering or coping with their experience.

This sensitivity undoubtedly contributed to Hughes's opening African-American poetry to everyday speech, popular art forms, and spirituality—

what contemporary critics sometimes call "the vernacular." Most important was the attention he paid to the multiple forms of African-influenced music in the United States: spirituals, blues, gospel, and jazz. Hughes discovered in this music not only a great reservoir of themes and characters for his poetry, but also a new approach to poetic diction and form, exemplified best perhaps in *Montage of a Dream Deferred* (1951).

Influenced by Walt Whitman, Carl Sandburg, and Paul Laurence Dunbar, Hughes's poetry is radically democratic. It celebrates the great diversity of American and African-American cultures and reveals the complexity of thought that persons of all backgrounds and in all stations in life hold. Perhaps more than any other American poet of his stature, Hughes sought to address the widest possible audience. He wrote children's books, plays and musicals for the Broadway stage, and a widely syndicated column for the African-American Chicago newspaper the *Defender*. For an extended short fiction series published in the *Defender,* the *Saturday Review,* and the *New York Post,* he created Jesse B. Semple, a character who in Hughes's stories was most often stationed at a Harlem bar stool, where he engaged in humorous dialogues with a somewhat more academic and demure narrator. Through this black Everyman, Hughes discussed art, politics, and the foibles of black and white people alike, in a manner that spoke down to no one.

For much of Hughes's life his commitment to a democratic art was combined with a willingness and zeal to confront racism and economic inequality directly. During the 1950s, changes in the political landscape led to an alteration in his rhetoric and the disappearance of much of the language of revolution in his poetry. While some of this change was probably due to the continued evolution of his political views, some of it was probably also due to his persecution during the McCarthy-era witch hunts. Nevertheless, there is a distinct continuity in his work; the political dimension to his poetry is consistent throughout his life. From the concrete expressions of black pride in the 1920s, through the challenges to poverty in the 1930s and 1940s, to his unequivocal enthusiasm and great sympathy for the Civil Rights movement in the late 1950s and 1960s, Hughes always wrote as if there were no question about the possibility of art to transform society. This idealism can be seen in the enthusiastic way Hughes documented the dramatic developments of the last decades of his life, in the poems that made up the posthumous *Panther and the Lash* (1967).

Contemporary critics and historians have often been at a loss to describe Hughes's poetic accomplishment. At mid-century a loose consensus began to develop that said poetry, especially in the classroom, should be difficult, indirect, and dense with allusions; Hughes's direct aesthetic philosophy and accessible poetry seemed distinctly out of step. The critical tendency has been to acknowledge Hughes as an important historical figure, but, unfortunately, not to study him in any depth. Today Hughes is best known for his striking individual poems of the 1920s, like "The Negro Speaks of Rivers" and "The Weary Blues," rather than for the experimentalism of books like *Shakespeare in Harlem* (1942) or *Ask Your Mama: Twelve Moods for Jazz* (1961). This is somewhat understandable given the great emotional power of the early poems. The great task for teachers and students of Langston Hughes, then, is to deal with the enormity of his intellectual ambition and the substantive ways in which he sought to challenge the conventions of American poetry and culture.

Literature

A Selection of Poems
by Langston Hughes

The Negro Speaks of Rivers
(1925)

I've known rivers:
I've known rivers ancient as the world and older than the
     flow of human blood in human veins.

My soul has grown deep like the rivers.

I bathed in the Euphrates[1] when dawns were young.
I built my hut near the Congo[2] and it lulled me to sleep.
I looked upon the Nile and raised the pyramids above it.
I heard the singing of the Mississippi when Abe Lincoln
       went down to New Orleans, and I've seen its muddy
       bosom turn all golden in the sunset.

I've known rivers:
Ancient, dusky rivers.

My soul has grown deep like the rivers.

---

[1] Major river of southwest Asia; with the Tigris, the Euphrates forms a valley sometimes
referred to as the "cradle of civilization."

[2] River in equatorial Africa, the continent's second longest.

The Weary Blues
(1925)

Droning a drowsy syncopated tune,
Rocking back and forth to a mellow croon,
  I heard a Negro play.
Down on Lenox Avenue[3] the other night
By the pale dull pallor of an old gas light
  He did a lazy sway . . .
  He did a lazy sway . . .
To the tune o' those Weary Blues.
With his ebony hands on each ivory key
He made that poor piano moan with melody.
  O Blues!
Swaying to and fro on his rickety stool
He played that sad raggy tune like a musical fool.
  Sweet Blues!
Coming from a black man's soul.
  O Blues!
In a deep song voice with a melancholy tone
I heard that Negro sing, that old piano moan—
  "Ain't got nobody in all this world,
  Ain't got nobody but ma self.
  I's gwine to quit ma frownin'
  And put ma troubles on the shelf."

Thump, thump, thump, went his foot on the floor.
He played a few chords then he sang some more—
  "I got the Weary Blues
  And I can't be satisfied.
  Got the Weary Blues
  And can't be satisfied—
  I ain't happy no mo'
  And I wish that I had died."
And far into the night he crooned that tune.
The stars went out and so did the moon.
The singer stopped playing and went to bed
While the Weary Blues echoed through his head.
He slept like a rock or a man that's dead.

---

[3] Street in Harlem, noted for nightlife and music during the 1920s.

I, Too
(1925)

I, too, sing America.

I am the darker brother.
They send me to eat in the kitchen
When company comes,
But I laugh,
And eat well,
And grow strong.

Tomorrow,
I'll be at the table
When company comes.
Nobody'll dare
Say to me,
"Eat in the kitchen,"
Then.

Besides,
They'll see how beautiful I am
And be ashamed—

I, too, am America.

Let America Be America Again
(1936)

Let America be America again.
Let it be the dream it used to be.
Let it be the pioneer on the plain
Seeking a home where he himself is free.

(America never was America to me.)

Let America be the dream the dreamers dreamed—
Let it be that great strong land of love
Where never kings connive nor tyrants scheme
That any man be crushed by one above.

(It never was America to me.)

O, let my land be a land where Liberty
Is crowned with no false patriotic wreath,
But opportunity is real, and life is free,
Equality is in the air we breathe.

(There's never been equality for me,
Nor freedom in this "homeland of the free.")

Say, who are you that mumbles in the dark?
And who are you that draws your veil across the stars?

I am the poor white, fooled and pushed apart,
I am the Negro bearing slavery's scars.
I am the red man driven from the land,
I am the immigrant clutching the hope I seek—
And finding only the same old stupid plan
Of dog eat dog, of mighty crush the weak.

I am the young man, full of strength and hope,
Tangled in that ancient endless chain
Of profit, power, gain, of grab the land!
Of grab the gold! Of grab the ways of satisfying need!
Of work the men! Of take the pay!
Of owning everything for one's own greed!

I am the farmer, bondsman to the soil.
I am the worker sold to the machine.
I am the Negro, servant to you all.
I am the people, humble, hungry, mean—
Hungry yet today despite the dream.
Beaten yet today—O, Pioneers!
I am the man who never got ahead,
The poorest worker bartered through the years.

Yet I'm the one who dreamt our basic dream
In that Old World while still a serf of kings,
Who dreamt a dream so strong, so brave, so true,
That even yet its mighty daring sings
In every brick and stone, in every furrow turned
That's made America the land it has become.
O, I'm the man who sailed those early seas
In search of what I meant to be my home—
For I'm the one who left dark Ireland's shore,
And Poland's plain, and England's grassy lea,
And torn from Black Africa's stand I came
To build a "homeland of the free."

The free?

Who said the free? Not me?
Surely not me? The millions on relief today?
The millions shot down when we strike?
The millions who have nothing for our pay?
For all the dreams we've dreamed
And all the songs we've sung
And all the hopes we've held
And all the flags we've hung,
The millions who have nothing for our pay—
Except the dream that's almost dead today.

O, let America be America again—
The land that never has been yet—
And yet must be—the land where *every* man is free.
The land that's mine—the poor man's, Indian's, Negro's, ME—
Who made America,

Whose sweat and blood, whose faith and pain,
Whose hand at the foundry, whose plow in the rain,
Must bring back our mighty dream again.

Sure, call me any ugly name you choose—
The steel of freedom does not stain.
From those who live like leeches on the people's lives,
We must take back our land again,
America!
O, yes,
I say it plain,
America never was America to me,
And yet I swear this oath—
America will be!

Out of the rack and ruin of our gangster death,
The rape and rot of graft, and stealth, and lies,
We, the people, must redeem
The land, the mines, the plants, the rivers.
The mountains and the endless plain—
All, all the stretch of these great green states—
And make America again!

Ballad of a Landlord
(1940)

Landlord, landlord,
My roof has sprung a leak.
Don't you 'member I told you about it
Way last week?

Landlord, landlord,
These steps is broken down.
When you come up yourself
It's a wonder you don't fall down.

Ten Bucks you say I owe you?
Ten Bucks you say is due?
Well, that's Ten Bucks more'n I'll pay you
Till you fix this house up new.

What? You gonna get eviction orders?
You gonna cut off my heat?
You gonna take my furniture and
Throw it in the street?

Um-huh! You talking high and mighty.
Talk on—till you get through.
You ain't gonna be able to say a word
If I land my fist on you.

Police! Police!
Come and get this man!
He's trying to ruin the government
And overturn the land!

Copper's whistle!
Patrol bell!
Arrest.

Precinct Station.
Iron cell.
Headlines in press:

MAN THREATENS LANDLORD

. .

TENANT HELD NO BAIL

. .

JUDGE GIVES NEGRO 90 DAYS IN COUNTY JAIL

Theme for English B
(1949)

The instructor said,

> *Go home and write*
> *a page tonight.*
> *And let that page come out of you—*
> *Then, it will be true.*

I wonder if it's that simple?
I am twenty-two, colored, born in Winston-Salem.
I went to school there, then Durham, then here
to this college on the hill above Harlem.
I am the only colored student in my class.
The steps from the hill lead down into Harlem,
through a park, then I cross St. Nicholas,
Eighth Avenue, Seventh, and I come to the Y,
the Harlem Branch Y, where I take the elevator
up to my room, sit down and write this page:

It's not easy to know what is true for you or me
at twenty-two, my age. But I guess I'm what
I feel and see and hear, Harlem, I hear you:
hear you, hear me—we two—you, me, talk on this page.
(I hear New York, too) Me—who?
Well, I like to eat, sleep, drink, and be in love.
I like to work, read, learn, and understand life.
I like a pipe for a Christmas present,
or records—Bessie,[4] bop,[5] or Bach.
I guess being colored doesn't make me *not* like
the same things other folks like who are other races.
So will my page be colored that I write?
Being me, it will not be white.

---

[4] Bessie Smith, blues singer, 1894–1937.

[5] Short for "bebop," a jazz style developed in the early 1940s by Charlie Parker, Dizzy
Gillespie, and others.

But it will be
a part of you, instructor.
You are white—
yet a part of me, as I am a part of you.
That's American.
Sometimes perhaps you don't want to be a part of me.
Nor do I often want to be a part of you.
But we are, that's true!
As I learn from you,
I guess you learn from me—
although you're older—and white—
and somewhat more free.

This is my page for English B.

Dream Boogie
(1951)

Good morning, daddy!
Ain't you heard
The boogie-woogie[6] rumble
Of a dream deferred?

Listen closely:
You'll hear their feet
Beating out and beating out a—

> *You think*
> *It's a happy beat?*

Listen to it closely:
Ain't you heard
something underneath
like a—

> *What did I say?*

Sure,
I'm happy!
Take it away!

> *Hey, pop!*
> *Re-bop!*
> *Mop!*

> *Y-e-a-h!*

---

[6] A popular black musical style with variants in both blues and jazz; more specifically, a vigorous piano style marked by heavy and repeated bass figures. Some commentators have also suggested that it was slang for syphilis.

Harlem
(1951)

What happens to a dream deferred?

Does it dry up
like a raisin in the sun?
Or fester like a sore—
And then run?
Does it stink like rotten meat?
Or crust and sugar over—
like a syrupy sweet?

Maybe it just sags
like a heavy load.

Or does it explode?

Birmingham Sunday (September 15, 1963)[7]
(1967)

Four little girls
Who went to Sunday School that day
And never came back home at all
But left instead
Their blood upon the wall
With spattered flesh
And bloodied Sunday dresses
Torn to shreds by dynamite
That China made aeons ago—
Did not know
That what China made
Before China was ever Red at all
Would redden with their blood
This Birmingham-on-Sunday wall.

Four tiny girls
Who left their blood upon that wall,
In little graves today await
The dynamite that might ignite
The fuse of centuries of Dragon Kings[8]
Whose tomorrow sings a hymn
The missionaries never taught Chinese
In Christian Sunday School
To implement the Golden Rule.

Four little girls
Might be awakened someday soon
By songs upon the breeze
As yet unfelt among magnolia trees.

---

[7] On this date, only weeks after Martin Luther King, Jr.'s historic March on Washington, DC, four young black girls were killed at their Sunday School in Birmingham, Alabama, by a bomb, likely in response to recent Civil Rights organizing in the area. The case has never been fully solved.

[8] In Chinese myth and lore the dragon is a beneficent force that dispenses blessings in both the natural and supernatural worlds. Eventually the dragon became a symbol of imperial China. Ironically, the dragon has also been utilized in the mythology of white supremacist groups like the Ku Klux Klan.

Discussion Questions

1. How do the historical and geographic allusions contribute to the power of "The Negro Speaks of Rivers"?

2. In what ways does Hughes use music and musical allusions? Are they "background" to the poems? Are the poems themselves meant to be musical?

3. Which of the poems strike you as being specifically poems of protest? Do any of the poems seem to hold aesthetic concerns secondary to social or political goals?

4. Is the question of identity (and especially racial identity) handled differently in "The Negro Speaks of Rivers" and "Theme for English B"? Do these poems espouse compatible philosophies?

5. How would you characterize Hughes's attitude to America as expressed in poems like "Let America Be America Again" and "I, Too"? Could he be considered a patriot?

6. Hughes is often celebrated for his ability to communicate complex human dilemmas in accessible language and forms. Evaluate his accomplishment in this regard in "Harlem."

7. Given the horror of the event that precipitated the poem "Birmingham Sunday," why does Hughes include indirect statements about Chinese mythology and history instead of a narrative treatment of events such as that in "Ballad of a Landlord"? What does his obliqueness accomplish?

8. Is the nature or character of dreaming identical in "Harlem" and "Dream Boogie"? Do you think the poems were meant to be read side by side? Or do they represent significantly different approaches to similar problems?

9. A strong "I" addresses readers in some of these poems. In which poems do you think the first person voice is explicitly autobiographical? In which poems is Hughes simply creating a dramatic speaker?

10. What do you think Hughes expects of readers of his poetry? Action? Reflection? A change of heart?

Research Questions

1. As Hughes's own essays in this volume suggest, much of his life was spent actively campaigning for various causes. Research further the nature of his commitments and their effect on his poetry. How was the nature of his social and political work different in 1935 and in 1955?

2. Using books like Leroi Jones's *Blues People* or Albert Murray's *Stomping the Blues* as sources, investigate the ways in which Hughes's poetry took inspiration from the accomplishments of African-American musicians. How might the different musical forms of, say, the female blues singers of the 1920s and the bebop musicians of the 1940s have inspired and directed Hughes?

3. Hughes was a primary inspiration for the artistic movement known as "negritude." Poets and writers like Nicolás Guillén, Jacques Roumain, Aimé Cesaire, and Leopold Senghor all acknowledged Hughes's influence. Find out what the "negritude" poets stood for and consider why Hughes would have been so important to their development.

4. Hughes's work was distinct from that of his two most important peers, Gwendolyn Brooks and Robert Hayden. Find a collection of the work of either of these writers, and compare their work to that of Hughes. These writers are sometimes distinguished from Hughes by noting the impact of "modernism" on Brooks and Hayden. Using a dictionary or an encyclopedia of literary criticism, find out what modernist poetry is. Is "modernism" a useful term in discussing what distinguishes Brooks and Hayden from Hughes? Why would Hughes be skeptical about some aspects of modernism?

5. George Hutchinson's article in this casebook talks about the influence of Walt Whitman on Hughes. Read some of the Whitman poems that Hutchinson argues were important to Hughes, and develop your own conclusions about what Hughes might have learned from Whitman. What do you think Hughes would have rejected in Whitman's work?

6. Read a collection of Hughes's "Simple Stories." Are his accomplishments in verse and fiction of a similar quality? What is he able to do in fiction that he is unable to do in poetry? What is he able to do in poetry that he is unable to do in fiction?

Secondary Sources

The materials offered in this section offer specific insights into the formation of particular Hughes poems and more general commentary on his development and importance as a poet. The first four sources are remarks made by Hughes which describe the social context within which he wrote. The fifth is an example of his fiction that illuminates further Hughes's straightforward and accessible style. The remaining sources are scholarly essays that consider particular problems or questions raised by Hughes's life and work. Use the essays to help generate writing ideas or to shape your own ideas for furthering the scholarly debate. You will also find materials in the Bibliography at the end of this book to supplement or extend your research interests. Remember that it is an absolute necessity that all borrowing of words and ideas be properly documented.

LANGSTON HUGHES

The Negro Artist and the Racial Mountain
(1926)

One of the most promising of the young Negro poets said to me once, "I want to be a poet—not a Negro poet," meaning, I believe, "I want to write like a white poet": meaning subconsciously, "I would like to be a white poet," meaning behind that, "I would like to be white." And I was sorry the young man said that, for no great poet has ever been afraid of being himself. And I doubted then that, with his desire to run away spiritually from his race, this boy would ever be a great poet. But this is the mountain standing in the way of any true Negro art in America—this urge within the race toward whiteness, the desire to pour racial individuality into the mold of American standardization, and to be as little Negro and as much American as possible.

But let us look at the immediate background of this young poet. His family is of what I suppose one would call the Negro middle class: people who are by no means rich yet never uncomfortable nor hungry—smug, contented, respectable folk, members of the Baptist church. The father goes to work every morning. He is a chief steward at a large white club. The mother sometimes does fancy sewing or supervises parties for the rich families of the town. The children go to a mixed school. In the home they read white papers and magazines. And the mother often says, "Don't be like niggers" when the children are bad. A frequent phrase from the father is, "Look how well a white man does things." And so the word white comes to be unconsciously a symbol of all the virtues. It holds for the children beauty, morality, and money. The whisper of "I want to be white" runs silently through their minds. This young poet's home is, I believe, a fairly typical home of the colored middle class. One sees immediately how difficult it would be for an artist born in such a home to interest himself in interpreting the beauty of his own people. He is never taught to see that beauty. He is taught rather not to see it, or if he does, to be ashamed of it when it is not according to Caucasian patterns.

For racial culture the home of a self-styled "high-class" Negro has nothing better to offer. Instead there will perhaps be more aping of things white than in a less cultured or less wealthy home. The father is perhaps a doctor, lawyer, landowner, or politician. The mother may be a social worker, or a teacher, or she may do nothing and have a maid. Father is often dark but he has usually married the lightest woman he could find. The family attend a fashionable church where few really colored faces are to be found. And they themselves draw a color line. In the North they go to white theaters and white movies. And in the South they have at least two cars and a house "like white folks." Nordic manners, Nordic faces, Nordic hair, Nordic art (if any), and an Episcopal heaven. A very high mountain indeed for the would-be racial artist to climb in order to discover himself and his people.

But then there are the low-down folks, the so-called common element, and they are the majority—may the Lord be praised! The people who have their nip of gin on Saturday nights are not too important to themselves or the community, or too well fed, or too learned to watch the lazy world go round. They live on Seventh Street in Washington or State Street in Chicago and they do not particularly care whether they are like white folks or anybody else. Their joy runs, bang! into ecstasy. Their religion soars to a shout. Work maybe a little today, rest a little tomorrow. Play awhile. Sing awhile. O, let's dance! These common people are not afraid of spirituals, as for a long time their more intellectual brethren were, and jazz is their child. They furnish a wealth of colorful, distinctive material for any artist because they still hold their own individuality in the face of American standardizations. And perhaps these common people will give to the world its truly great Negro artist, the one who is not afraid to be himself. Whereas the better-class Negro would tell the artist what to do, the people at least let him alone when he does appear. And they are not ashamed of him—if they know he exists at all. And they accept what beauty is their own without question.

Certainly there is, for the American Negro artist who can escape the restrictions the more advanced among his own group would put upon him, a great field of unused material ready for his art. Without going outside his race, and even among the better classes with their "white" culture and conscious American manners, but still Negro enough to be different, there is sufficient matter to furnish a black artist with a lifetime of creative work. And when he chooses to touch on the relations between Negroes and whites in this country with their innumerable overtones and undertones, surely, and especially for literature and the drama, there is an inexhaustible supply of themes at hand. To these the Negro artist can give his racial individuality, his heritage of rhythm and warmth, and his incongruous humor that so often, as in the Blues, becomes ironic laughter mixed with tears. But let us look again at the mountain.

A prominent Negro clubwoman in Philadelphia paid eleven dollars to hear Raquel Meller sing Andalusian popular songs. But she told me a few weeks before she would not think of going to hear "that woman," Clara Smith, a great black artist, sing Negro folksongs. And many an upper-class Negro church, even now, would not dream of employing a spiritual in its services. The drab melodies in white folks' hymnbooks are much to be preferred. "We want to worship the Lord correctly and quietly. We don't believe in 'shouting.' "Let's be dull like the Nordics," they say, in effect.

The road for the serious black artist, then, who would produce a racial art is most certainly rocky and the mountain is high. Until recently he received almost no encouragement for his work from either white or colored people. The fine novels of Chesnutt go out of print with neither race noticing their passing. The quaint charm and humor of Dunbar's dialect verse brought to him, in his day, largely the same kind of encouragement one would give a side-show freak (A colored man writing poetry! How odd!) or a clown (How amusing!).

The present vogue in things Negro, although it may do as much harm as good for the budding colored artist, has at least done this: it has brought him forcibly to the attention of his own people among whom for so long, unless the other race had noticed him beforehand, he was a prophet with little honor. I understand that Charles Gilpin acted for years in Negro theaters without any special acclaim from his own, but when Broadway gave him eight curtain calls, Negroes, too, began to beat a tin pan in his honor. I know a young colored writer, a manual worker by day, who had been writing well for the colored magazines for some years, but it was not until he recently broke into the white publications and his first book was accepted by a prominent New York publisher that the "best" Negroes in his city took the trouble to discover that he lived there. Then almost immediately they decided to give a grand dinner for him. But the society ladies were careful to whisper to his mother that perhaps she'd better not come. They were not sure she would have an evening gown.

The Negro artist works against an undertow of sharp criticism and misunderstanding from his own group and unintentional bribes from the whites. "O, be respectable, write about nice people, show how good we are," say the Negroes. "Be stereotyped, don't go too far, don't shatter our illusions about you, don't amuse us too seriously. We will pay you," say the whites. Both would have told Jean Toomer not to write *Cane*. The colored people did not praise it. The white people did not buy it. Most of the colored people who did read *Cane* hate it. They are afraid of it. Although the critics gave it good reviews the public remained indifferent. Yet (excepting the work of DuBois) *Cane* contains the finest prose written by a Negro in America. And like the singing of Robeson, it is truly racial.

But in spite of the Nordicized Negro intelligentsia and the desires of some white editors, we have an honest American Negro literature already with us. Now await the rise of the Negro theater. Our folk music, having achieved world-wide fame, offers itself to the genius of the great individual American Negro composer who is to come. And within the next decade I expect to see the work of a growing school of colored artists who paint and model the beauty of dark faces and create with new technique the expressions of their own soul-world. And the Negro dancers who will dance like flame and the singers who will continue to carry out songs to all who listen—they will be with us in even greater numbers tomorrow.

Most of my own poems are racial in theme and treatment, derived from the life I know. In many of them I try to grasp and hold some of the meanings and rhythms of jazz. I am sincere as I know how to be in these poems and yet after every reading I answer questions like these from my own people: Do you think Negroes should always write about Negroes? I wish you wouldn't read some of your poems to white folks. How do you find anything interesting in a place like a cabaret? Why do you write about black people? You aren't black. What makes you do so many jazz poems?

But jazz to me is one of the inherent expressions of Negro life in America: the eternal tom-tom beating in the Negro soul—the tom-tom of revolt against weariness in a white world, a world of subway trains, and work, work, work; the tom-tom of joy and laughter, and pain swallowed in a smile. Yet the Philadelphia clubwoman is ashamed to say that her race created it and she does not like me to write about it. The old subconscious "white is best" runs through her mind. Years of study under white teachers, a lifetime of white books, pictures, and papers, and white manners, morals, and Puritan standards made her dislike the spirituals. And now she turns up her nose at jazz and all its manifestations—likewise almost everything else distinctly racial. She doesn't care for the Winold Reiss portraits of Negroes because they are "too Negro." She does not want a true picture of herself from anybody. She wants the artist to flatter her, to make the white world believe that all Negroes are as smug and as near white in soul as she wants to be. But, to my mind, it is the duty of the younger Negro artist, if he accepts any duties at all from outsiders, to change through the force of his art that old whispering "I want to be white," hidden in the aspirations of his people, to "Why should I want to be white? I am a Negro—and beautiful!"

So I am ashamed for the black poet who says, "I want to be a poet, not a Negro poet," as though his own racial world were not as interesting as any other world. I am ashamed, too, for the colored artist who runs from the painting of Negro faces to the painting of sunsets after the manner of the academicians because he fears the strange un-whiteness of his own features. An artist must be free to choose what he does, certainly, but he must also never be afraid to do what he might choose.

Let the blare of Negro jazz bands and the bellowing voice of Bessie Smith singing Blues penetrate the closed ears of the colored near-intellectuals until they listen and perhaps understand. Let Paul Robeson singing Water Boy, and Rudolph Fisher writing about the streets of Harlem, and Jean Toomer holding the heart of Georgia in his hands, and Aaron Douglas drawing strange black fantasies cause the smug Negro middle class to turn from their white, respectable, ordinary books and papers to catch a glimmer of their own beauty. We younger Negro artists who create now intend to express our individual dark-skinned selves without fear or shame. If white people are pleased we are glad. If they are not, it doesn't matter. We know we are beautiful. And ugly too. The tom-tom cries and the tom-tom laughs. If colored people are pleased we are glad. If they are not, their displeasure doesn't matter either. We build our temples for tomorrow, strong as we know how, and we stand on top of the mountain, free within ourselves.

LANGSTON HUGHES

To Negro Writers
(1935)

There are certain practical things American Negro writers can do through their work.

We can reveal to the Negro masses, from which we come, our potential power to transform the now ugly face of the Southland into a region of peace and plenty.

We can reveal to the white masses those Negro qualities which go beyond the mere ability to laugh and sing and dance and make music, and which are a part of the useful heritage that we place at the disposal of a future free America.

Negro writers can seek to unite blacks and whites in our country, not on the nebulous basis of an inter-racial meeting, or the shifting sands of religious brotherhood, but on the *solid* ground of the daily working-class struggle to wipe out, now and forever, all the old inequalities of the past.

Furthermore, by way of exposure, Negro writers can reveal in their novels, stories, poems, and articles:

The lovely grinning face of Philanthropy—which gives a million dollars to a Jim Crow school, but not one job to a graduate of that school; which builds a Negro hospital with second-rate equipment, then commands black patients and student-doctors to go there whether they will or no; or which, out of the kindness of its heart, erects yet another separate, segregated, shut-off, Jim Crow Y.M.C.A.

Negro writers can expose those white labor leaders who keep their unions closed against Negro workers and prevent the betterment of all workers.

We can expose, too, the sick-sweet smile of organized religion—which lies about what it doesn't know, and about what it *does* know. And the half-voodoo, half-clown, face of revivalism, dulling the mind with the clap of its empty hands.

Expose, also, the false leadership that besets the Negro people—bought and paid for leadership, owned by capital, afraid to open its mouth except in the old conciliatory way so advantageous to the exploiters.

And all the economic roots of race hatred and race fear.

And the Contentment Tradition of the O-lovely-Negroes school of American fiction, which makes an ignorant black face and a Carolina head filled with superstition, appear more desirable than a crown of gold; the jazz-band; and the O-so-gay writers who make of the Negro's poverty and misery a dusky funny paper.

And expose war. And the old My-Country-'Tis-of-Thee lie. And the colored American Legion posts strutting around talking about the privilege of dying for the nobel Red, White and Blue, when they aren't even permitted the privilege of living for it. Or voting for it in Texas. Or working for it in the diplomatic service. Or even rising, like every other good little boy, from the log cabin to the White House.

White House is right!

Dear colored American Legion, you can swing from a lynching tree, uniform and all, with pleasure—and nobody'll fight for you. Don't you know that? Nobody even salutes you down South, dead or alive, medals or no medals, chevrons or not, no matter how many wars you've fought in.

Let Negro writers write about the irony and pathos of the *colored* American Legion.

> *"Salute, Mr. White Man!"*
> "Salute, hell! . . . You're a nigger."

Or would you rather write about the moon?

Sure, the moon still shines over Harlem. Shines over Scottsboro. Shines over Birmingham, too, I reckon. Shines over Cordie Cheek's grave, down South.

Write about the moon if you want to. Go ahead. This is a free country.

But there are certain very practical things American Negro writers can do. And must do. There's a song that says, "the time ain't long." That song is right. Something has got to change in America—and change soon. We must help that change to come.

The moon's still shining as poetically as ever, but all the stars on the flag are dull. (And the stripes, too.)

We want a new and better America, where there won't be any poor, where there won't be any more Jim Crow, where there won't be any lynchings, where there won't be any munition makers, where we won't need philanthropy, nor charity, nor the New Deal, nor Home Relief.

We want an America that will be ours, a world that will be ours—we Negro workers and white workers! Black writers and white! We'll make that world!

LANGSTON HUGHES

My Adventures as a Social Poet
(1947)

Poets who write mostly about love, roses and moonlight, sunsets and snow, must lead a very quiet life. Seldom, I imagine, does their poetry get them into difficulties. Beauty and lyricism are really related to another world, to ivory towers, to your head in the clouds, feet floating off the earth.

Unfortunately, having been born poor—and also colored—in Missouri, I was stuck in the mud from the beginning. Try as I might to float off into the clouds, poverty and Jim Crow would grab me by the heels, and right back on earth I would land. A third-floor furnished room is the nearest thing I have ever had to an ivory tower.

Some of my earliest poems were social poems in that they were about people's problems—whole groups of people's problems—rather than my own personal difficulties. Sometimes, though, certain aspects of my personal problems happened to be also common to many other people. And certainly, racially speaking, my own problems of adjustment to American life were the same as those of millions of other segregated Negroes. The moon belongs to everybody, but not this American earth of ours. That is perhaps why poems about the moon perturb no one, but poems about color and poverty do perturb many citizens. Social forces pull backwards or forwards, right or left, and social poems get caught in the pulling and hauling. Sometimes the poet himself gets pulled and hauled—even hauled off to jail.

I have never been in jail but I have been detained by the Japanese police in Tokyo and by the immigration authorities in Cuba—in custody, to put it politely—due, no doubt, to their interest in my written words. These authorities would hardly have detained me had I been a writer of the roses and moonlight school. I have never known the police of any country to show an interest in lyric poetry as such. But when poems stop talking about the moon and begin to mention poverty, trade unions, color lines, and colonies, somebody tells the police. The history of world literature has many examples of poets fleeing into exile to escape persecution, of poets in jail, even of poets killed like Placido or, more recently, Lorca in Spain.

My adventures as a social poet are mild indeed compared to the body-breaking, soul-searing experiences of poets in the recent Fascist countries or of the resistance poets of the Nazi-invaded lands during the war. For that reason, I can use so light a word as "adventure" in regard to my own skirmishes with reaction and censorship.

My adventures as a social poet began in a colored church in Atlantic City shortly after my first book, *The Weary Blues,* was published in 1926. I had been invited to come down to the shore from Lincoln University where I was a student, to give a program of my poems in the church. During the course of my program I read several of my poems in the form of the Negro folk songs, including some blues poems about hard luck and hard work. As I read I noticed a deacon approach the pulpit with a note which he placed on the rostrum beside me, but I did not stop to open the note until I had finished and had acknowledged the applause of a cordial audience. The note read, "Do not read any more blues in my pulpit." It was signed by the minister. That was my first experience with censorship.

The kind and generous woman who sponsored my writing for a few years after my college days did not come to the point quite so directly as did the minister who disliked blues. Perhaps, had it not been in the midst of the great depression of the late '20's and early '30's, the kind of poems that I am afraid helped to end her patronage might not have been written. But it was impossible for me to travel from hungry Harlem to the lovely homes on Park Avenue without feeling in my soul the great gulf between the very poor and the very rich in our society. In those days, on the way to visit this kind lady I would see the homeless sleeping in subways and the hungry begging in doorways on sleet-stung winter days. It was then that I wrote a poem called "Advertisement for the Waldorf-Astoria," satirizing the slick-paper magazine advertisements of the opening of that de luxe hotel. Also I wrote:

PARK BENCH

I live on a park bench,
You, Park Avenue.
Hell of a distance
Between us two.

I beg a dime for dinner—
You got a butler and maid.
But I'm wakin' up!
Say, ain't you afraid

That I might, just maybe,
In a year or two,
Move on over
To Park Avenue?

In a little while I did not have a patron any more.

But that year I won a prize, the Harmon Gold Award for Literature, which consisted of a medal and four hundred dollars. With the four hundred dollars I went to Haiti. On the way I stopped in Cuba and I was cordially received by the writers and artists. I had written poems about the exploitation of Cuba by the sugar barons and I had translated many poems of Nicolás Guillén such as:

CANE

Negro
In the cane fields.
White man
Above the cane fields
Earth
Beneath the cane fields.
Blood
That flows from us.

This was during the days of the dictatorial Machado regime. Perhaps someone called his attention to these poems and translations because, when I came back from Haiti weeks later, I was not allowed to land in Cuba, but was detained by the immigration authorities at Santiago and put on an island until the American consul came, after three days, to get me off with the provision that I cross the country to Havana and leave Cuban soil at once.

That was my first time being put out of any place. But since that time I have been put out of or barred from quite a number of places, all because of my poetry—not the roses and moonlight poems (which I write, too) but because of poems about poverty, oppression, and segregation. Nine Negro boys in Alabama were on trial for their lives when I got back from Cuba and Haiti. The famous Scottsboro "rape" case was in full session. I visited those boys in the death house at Kilby Prison, and I wrote many poems about them. One of these poems was:

CHRIST IN ALABAMA

Christ is a Nigger,
Beaten and black—
O, bare your back.

Mary is His Mother—
Mammy of the South,
Silence your mouth.

God's His Father—
White Master above,
Grant us your love.

Most holy bastard
Of the bleeding mouth:
Nigger Christ
On the cross of the South.

Contempo, a publication of some of the students at the University of North Carolina, published the poem on its front page on the very day that I was being presented in a program of my poems at the University in Chapel Hill. That evening there were police outside the building in which I spoke, and in the air the rising tension of race that is peculiar to the South. It had been rumored that some of the local citizenry were saying that I should be run out of town, and that one of the sheriffs agreed, saying, "Sure, he ought to be run out! It's bad enough to call Christ a *bastard.* But when he calls him a *nigger,* he's gone too far!"

The next morning a third of my fee was missing when I was handed my check. One of the departments of the university jointly sponsoring my program had refused to come through with its portion of the money. Nevertheless, I remember with pleasure the courtesy and kindness of many of the students and faculty at Chapel Hill and their lack of agreement with the anti-Negro elements of the town. There I began to learn at the University of North Carolina how hard it is to be a white liberal in the South.

It was not until I had been to Russia and around the world as a writer and journalist that censorship and opposition to my poems reached the point of completely preventing me from appearing in public programs on a few occasions. It happened first in Los Angeles shortly after my return from the Soviet Union. I was to have been one of several speakers on a memorial program to be held at the colored branch Y.M.C.A. for a young Negro journalist of the community. At the behest of white higher-ups, no doubt, some reactionary Negro politicians informed the Negro Y.M.C.A. that I was a Communist. The secretary of the Negro Branch Y then informed the committee of young people in charge of the memorial that they could have their program only if I did not appear.

I have never been a Communist, but I soon learned that anyone visiting the Soviet Union and speaking with favor of it upon returning is liable to be so labeled. Indeed when Mrs. Roosevelt, Walter White, and so Christian a lady as Mrs. Bethune who has never been in Moscow, are so labeled, I should hardly be surprised! I wasn't surprised. And the young people's committee informed the Y secretary that since the Y was a public community center which they helped to support, they saw no reason why it should censor their memorial program to the extent of eliminating any speaker.

Since I had been allotted but a few moments on the program, it was my intention simply to read this short poem of mine:

Dear lovely death
That taketh all things under wing,
Never to kill,
Only to change into some other thing
This suffering flesh—
To make it either more or less
But not again the same,
Dear lovely death,
Change is thy other name.

But the Negro branch Y, egged on by the reactionary politicians (whose incomes, incidentally, were allegedly derived largely from gambling houses and other underworld activities), informed the young people's committee that the police would be at the door to prevent my entering the Y on the afternoon of the scheduled program. So when the crowd gathered, the memorial was not held that Sunday. The young people simply informed the audience of the situation and said that the memorial would be postponed until a place could be found where all the participants could be heard. The program was held elsewhere a few Sundays later.

Somebody with malice aforethought (probably the Negro politicians of Uncle Tom vintage) gave the highly publicized California evangelist, Aimee Semple McPherson, a copy of a poem of mine, "Goodbye, Christ." This poem was one of my least successful efforts at poetic communication, in that many persons have misinterpreted it as an anti-Christian poem. I intended it to be just the opposite. Satirical, even ironic, in style, I meant it to be a poem against those whom I felt were misusing religion for worldly or profitable purposes. In the poem I mentioned Aimee Semple McPherson. This apparently made her angry. From her Angelus Temple pulpit she preached against me, saying, "There are many devils among us, but the most dangerous of all is the red devil. And now there comes among us a red devil *in a black skin!*"

She gathered her followers together and sent them to swoop down upon me one afternoon at an unsuspecting and innocent literary luncheon in Pasadena's Vista del Arroyo Hotel. Robert Nathan, I believe, was one of the speakers, along with a number of other authors. I was to have five minutes on the program to read a few poems from my latest collection of folk verses, *Shakespeare in Harlem,* hardly a radical book.

When I arrived at the hotel by car from Los Angeles, I noticed quite a crowd in the streets where the traffic seemed to be tangled. So I got out some distance from the front of the hotel and walked through the grounds to the entrance, requesting my car to return at three o'clock. When I asked in the lobby for the location of the luncheon, I was told to wait until the desk clerk sent for the chairman, George Palmer Putnam. Mr. Putnam arrived with the manager, both visibly excited. They informed me that the followers of Aimee McPherson were vehemently picketing the hotel because of my appearance there. The manager added with an aggrieved look that he could not have such a commotion in front of his hotel. Either I would have to go or he would cancel the entire luncheon.

Mr. Putnam put it up to me. I said that rather than inconvenience several hundred guests and a half dozen authors, I would withdraw—except that I did not know where my car had gone, so would someone be kind enough to drive me to the station. Just then a doorman came in to inform the manager that traffic was completely blocked in front of the hotel. Frantically the manager rushed out. About that time a group of Foursquare Gospel members poured into the lobby in uniforms and armbands and surrounded me and George Palmer Putnam demanding to know if we were Christians. Before I could say anything, Mr. Putnam lit into them angrily, saying it was none of their business and stating that under our Constitution a man could have any religion he chose, as well as freedom to express himself.

Just then an old gentleman [of] about seventy-two who was one of the organizers of the literary luncheon came up, saying he had been asked to drive me to the station and get me out of there so they could start the luncheon. Shaking hands with Mr. Putnam, I accompanied the old gentleman to the street. There Aimee's sound truck had been backed across the roadway blocking all passage so that limousines, trucks, and taxis were tangled up in all directions. The sound truck was playing "God Bless America" while hundreds of pickets milled about with signs denouncing Langston Hughes—atheistic Red. Rich old ladies on the arms of their chauffeurs were trying to get through the crowd to the luncheon. Reporters were dashing about.

None of the people recognized me, but in the excitement the old gentleman could not find his car. Finally he hailed a taxi and nervously thrust a dollar into the driver's hand with the request that I be driven to the station. He asked to be excused himself in order to get back to the luncheon. Just as I reached out the door to shake hands in farewell, three large white ladies with banners rushed up to the cab. One of them screamed, "We don't shake hands with niggers where we come from!"

The thought came over me that the picketing might turn into a race riot, in which case I did not wish to be caught in a cab in a traffic jam alone.

I did not turn loose the old gentleman's hand. Instead of shaking it in fare-well, I simply pulled him into the taxi with me, saying, "I thought you were going to the station, too."

As the pickets snarled outside, I slammed the door. The driver started off, but we were caught in the traffic blocked by the sound truck lustily play-ing "God Bless America." The old gentleman trembled beside me, until fi-nally we got clear of the mob. As we backed down a side street and turned to head for the station, the sirens of approaching police cars were heard in the distance.

Later I learned from the afternoon papers that the whole demonstration had been organized by Aimee McPherson's publicity man, and that when the police arrived he had been arrested for refusing to give up the keys to the sound truck stalled midway in the street to block the traffic. This simply proved the point I had tried to make in the poem—that the church might as well bid Christ goodbye if His gospel were left in the hands of such people.

Four years later I was to be picketed again in Detroit by Gerald L. K. Smith's Mothers of America—for ever since the Foursquare Gospel dem-onstration in California, reactionary groups have copied, used and distrib-uted this poem. Always they have been groups like Smith's, never known to help the fight for democratic Negro rights in America, but rather to use their energies to foment riots such as that before Detroit's Sojourner Truth hous-ing project where the Klanminded tried to prevent colored citizens from oc-cupying government homes built for them.

I have had one threatening communication signed *A Klansman*. And many scurrilous anonymous anti-Negro letters from persons whose writing did not always indicate illiteracy. On a few occasions, reactionary elements have forced liberal sponsors to cancel their plans to present me in a reading of my poems. I recall that in Gary, Indiana, some years ago the colored teachers were threatened with the loss of their jobs if I accepted their invi-tation to appear at one of the public schools. In another city a white high school principal, made apprehensive by a small group of reactionary parents, told me that he communicated with the F.B.I. at Washington to find out if I were a member of the Communist party. Assured that I was not, with the approval of his school board, he presented me to his study body. To further fortify his respectability, that morning at assembly, he had invited all of the Negro ministers and civic leaders of the town to sit on the stage in a semi-circle behind me. To the students it must have looked like a kind of modern minstrel show, as it was the first time any Negroes at all had been invited to their assembly.

So goes the life of social poet. I am sure none of these things would ever have happened to me had I limited the subject matter of my poems to roses and moonlight. But, unfortunately, I was born poor—and colored—and almost all the prettiest roses I have seen have been in rich white people's yards—not in mine. That is why I cannot write exclusively about roses and moonlight—for sometimes in the moonlight my brothers see a fiery cross and a circle of Klansmen's hoods. Sometimes in the moonlight a dark body sways from a lynching tree—but for his funeral there are no roses.

LANGSTON HUGHES

Langston Hughes Speaks
(1953)

During a period in my life coinciding roughly with the beginning of the Scottsboro Case and the depression of the 1930's and running through to the Nazi-Soviet Pact, I wrote a number of poems which reflected my then deep sympathies with certain of the aims and objectives of the leftist philosophies and the interests of the Soviet Union in the problem of poverty, minorities, colonial peoples, and particularly of Negroes and Jim Crow. Most of these poems appeared only in booklet form and have long been out of print. I was amazed to learn that some of these out-dated examples of my work are today being circulated in our State Department's overseas libraries. Written, some of them, partially in leftist terminology with the red flag as a symbol of freedom, they could hardly serve to present a contemporary picture of American ideals or of my personal ones.

I am not now and have never been a member of the Communist party, and have so stated over the years in my speeches and writings. But there is in my family a long history of participation in social struggle—from my grandfather who went to prison for helping slaves to freedom and another relative who died with John Brown at Harper's Ferry to my great uncle, John M. Langston, only Negro Representative in Congress from Virginia following the Reconstruction, and who had supported Abraham Lincoln in his recruiting Negro troops, and spoken for freedom on the same platform with Garrison and Phillips. In my own youth, faced with the problems of both poverty and color, and penniless at the beginning of the depression, I was strongly attracted by some of the promises of Communism, but always with the reservations, among others, of a creative writer wishing to preserve my own freedom of action and expression—and as an American Negro desiring full integration into our body politic. These two reservations—particularly (since I could never accept the totalitarian regimentation of the artist nor the Communist theory of a Negro state for the Black Belt)—were among other reasons why I never contemplated joining the Communist party, although various aspects of Communist interests were for some years reflected in the emotional content of my writing. But I was shocked at the Nazi-Soviet Pact, just as I am shocked now by the reported persecution of the Jewish people. And I was disturbed by the complete lack of freedom of press and publication I observed in the USSR. In our own country I have been greatly heartened in recent years by the progress being made in race-relations, by the recent Supreme Court decisions relative to Negro education, restrictive covenants, the ballot, and travel. My work of the war years, and my latest books have reflected this change of emphasis and development in my own thinking and orientation. This is, I think, clearly and simply shown in the last paragraph of my latest book [*The First Book of Negroes*]:

"Our country has many problems still to solve, but America is young, big, strong, and beautiful. And we are trying very hard to be, as the flag says, 'one nation, indivisible, with liberty and justice for all.' Here people are free to vote and work out their problems. In some countries people are governed by rulers, and ordinary folks can't do a thing about it. But here all of us are a part of democracy. By taking an interest in our government, and by treating our neighbors as we would like to be treated, each one of us can help make our country the most wonderful country in the world."

LANGSTON HUGHES

Swinging High
(1965)

"A meat ball by any other name is still a meat ball just the same," said Simple. "My wife, Joyce, is a fiend for foreign foods. Almost every time she drags me downtown to a show, she wants to go eat in some new kind of restaurant, Spanish, French, Greek, or who knows what? Last night we had something writ on the menu in a Philippine restaurant in big letters as BOLA-BOLAS. They returned out to be nothing but meat balls."

"*Bola* probably means 'ball' in their language," I said. "But I am like Joyce. I sort of go for foreign foods, too—something different once in a while, you know."

"Me, I like plain old down-home victuals, soul food with corn bread," said Simple, "spare ribs, pork chops, and things like that. Ham hock, string beans, salt pork and cabbage."

"All good foods," I said, "but for a change, why not try chicken curry and rootie next time you take Joyce out."

"What is that?" asked Simple.

"An East Indian dish, chicken stewed in curry sauce."

"I am not West Indian nor East," said Simple.

"You don't have to be foreign to like foreign food," I said.

"Left to me, I would go to Jenny Lou's up yonder on Seventh Avenue across from Small's Paradise. Jenny Lou's is where all the down-home folks eat when they is visiting Harlem. They knows good home-like food a mile away by the way it smells."

"A restaurant is not supposed to smell," I said. "The scent of cooking is supposed to be kept in the kitchen."

"Jenny Lou's kitchen is in the dining room," said Simple. "When I were a single man, I et there often. Them low prices suited my pocket."

"How about Frank's?" I asked. "Now Negro-owned."

"That's where Joyce takes her society friends like Mrs. Maxwell-Reeves," said Simple. "The menu is as big as newspaper. So many things on it, it is hard to know what to pick out. I like to just say 'pork chops' and be done with it. I don't want soup, neither salad. And who wants rice pudding for dessert? Leave off them things, also olives. Just give me pork chops."

"Is that all?"

"I'll take the gravy," Simple said.

"Pork chops, bread, and gravy," I shook my head. "As *country* as you can be!"

"If that is what you call *country,*" said Simple, "still gimme pork chops. Pork chops and fried apples maybe, if they is on the menu. I love fried apples, and my Uncle Tige had an apple tree in his back yard. When I was a little small boy, I used to set in a rope swing behind my Uncle Tige's house. The swing were attached to that apple tree which were a very old apple tree, and big for an apple tree, and a good tree for a swing for boys and girls. It were nice to set in this swing when I was yet a wee small boy and be pushed by the bigger children because I was still too small for my feet to touch the ground, and I did not know how to pump myself up into the air. Later I could. Later I could stand up in that swing and pump myself way up into the air, almost as high as the limb on which the swing were tied. Oh, I remember very well that swing and that apple tree when I were a child.

"It looks to me life is like a swing," continued Simple. "When young, somebody else must push you because your feet are too short to touch the ground and start the swing in motion. But later you go for yourself. By and by, you can stand up and swing high, swing high, way high up, and you are on your own. How wonderful it is to stand up in the swing, pumping all by yourself! But suppose the rope was to break, the tree limb snap off when you have pumped yourself up so high? Suppose it dies? You will be the one to fall, nobody else, just you yourself. Yes, life is like a swing! But in spite of all and everything, it is good to swing. Oh, yes! The swing of life is wonderful, but if you are a colored swinger, you have to have a stout heart, pump hard, and hold tight to get even a few feet above the ground. And be careful that your neighbor next door, white, has not cut your rope, so that just when you are swinging highest, it will break and throw you to the ground. 'Look at that Negro swinging! But he done fell!' they say. But someday we gonna swing right up to the very top of the tree and not fall. Yes, someday we will."

"Integrated, I hope," I said.

"Yes, integrated, I reckon," said Simple. "But some folks is getting so wrapped up in this integration thing, white and colored, that I do believe some of them is going stone-cold crazy. You see how here in New York peoples is talking to themselves on buses and in the subways, whirling around in the middle of the street, mumbling and grumbling all by themselves to nobody on park benches, dumping garbage on bridges, slicing up subway seats with knives and nail files, running out of gas on crowded highways on purpose and liable to get smashed up in traffic jams. Oh, I do not know what has come over the human race—like that nice young white minister in Cleveland laying down *behind* a rolling bulldozer, *not* in front of it—where the driver could see him and maybe stop in time before the man got crushed to death. He were protesting Jim Crow—but sometimes the protest is worse than the Crow."

"That earnest white man, no doubt, was trying to call attention to the urgency of the civil rights," I said. "He wanted to keep the movement on the front pages of the newspapers."

"It has been on the front pages of the newspapers for ten years," said Simple, "and if everybody does not know by now something needs to be done about civil rights, they will never know. After so many Freedom Rides and sit-ins and picketings and head bustings and police dogs and bombings and little children blowed up, and teenagers in jail by the thousands up to now, and big headlines across the newspapers, colored and white, why did that good white minister in Cleveland with his glasses on have to lay down *behind* a bulldozer?"

"I gather there are some things you would not do for a cause," I said.

"I would not lay down behind a bulldozer going backwards. How would my dying help anything—and my wife, Joyce, would be left a widow? It is not that I might be dying in a good cause, but let me die on my own two feet, knowing where, when, and why, and maybe making a speech telling off the world—not in a wreck because somebody has stalled a car whilst traffic is speeding. To me that is crazy! Whoever drives them stalled cars might be smashed up and killed too."

"They would consider themselves martyrs," I said.

"They should not make a martyr out of me in another car who do not even know them," said Simple. "Let me make a martyr out of myself, if I want to, but don't make me one under other peoples' cars. I do not want to be a martyr on nobody else's time. And don't roll no bulldozer over me unless I am standing in front, not behind it when it rolls. If I have got to look death in the face ahead of time, at least let me know who is driving. Also don't take me by surprise before I have paid my next year's dues to the NAACP. Anyhow, a car or a bulldozer is a dangerous thing to fool around with, as is any kind of moving machinery. You remember that old joke about the washer-woman who bent over too far and got both her breasts caught in the wringer? There is such a thing as bending over too far—even to get your clothes clean. Certainly there is plenty of dirty linen in this U.S.A., but I do not advise nobody to get their breast caught in a wringer. Machines do not have no sense."

"A cynic might say the same thing about martyrs," I said. "Except sometimes it takes an awful lot of sense to have no sense."

"Maybe you are right," said Simple, "just like it takes a mighty lot of pumping to swing high in the swing of life."

ARNOLD RAMPERSAD

The Origins of Poetry
in Langston Hughes
(1985)

In his study *The Life of the Poet: Beginning and Ending Poetic Careers* (1981) Lawrence Lipking asks three main questions, one of which concerns me here in the case of Langston Hughes: "How does an aspiring author of verses become a poet?" In the case of John Keats, for example, how did the poet arrive at "On First Looking Into Chapman's Homer," that great leap in creative ability in which Keats, sweeping from the legend of "the realms of gold" toward modern history, "catches sight not of someone else's dream but of his own reality? He stares at his future, and surmises that he may be a poet. The sense of possibility is thrilling, the moment truly awesome. Keats has discovered Keats." Or in the well-known words of Keats himself: "The Genius of Poetry must work out its own salvation in a man: It cannot be matured by law & precept, but by sensation & watchfulness in itself—That which is creative must create itself."

Can one ask a similar question about the origins of poetry in Langston Hughes, who in June 1921, at the age of nineteen, began a celebrated career when he published his own landmark poem "The Negro Speaks of Rivers" in W.E.B. Du Bois' *Crisis* magazine? Like Keats before "Chapman's Homer," Hughes had written poems before "The Negro Speaks of Rivers." Much of the poetry before "Rivers" is available for examination, since Hughes published steadily in the monthly magazine of his high school in Cleveland, Ohio. Certain aspects of this verse are noteworthy. It has nothing to do with race; it is dominated by images of the poet not as a teenager but as a little child; and, in Hughes's junior year, he published his first poem in free verse, one that showed the clear influence of Walt Whitman for the first (but not the last) time. Revealing an increase in skill, Hughes's early poetry nevertheless gives no sign of a major poetic talent in the making. At some point in his development, however, something happened to Hughes that was as mysterious and as wonderful, in its own way, as the miracle that overtook John Keats after the watchful night spent with his friend Charles Cowden Clarke and a copy of Chapman's translation. With "The Negro Speaks of Rivers" the creativity in Langston Hughes, hitherto unexpressed, suddenly created itself.

In writing thus about Hughes, are we taking him too seriously? With a few exceptions, literary critics have resisted offering even a modestly complicated theory concerning his creativity. His relentless affability and charm, his deep, open love of the black masses, his devotion to their folk forms, and his insistence on writing poetry that they could understand, all have contributed to the notion that Langston Hughes was intellectually and emotionally shallow. One wonders, then, at the source of the creative energy that drove him from 1921 to 1967 to write so many poems, novels, short stories, plays, operas, popular histories, children's books, and assorted other work. As a poet, Hughes virtually reinvented Afro-American poetry with his pioneering use of the blues and other folk forms; as Howard Mumford Jones

marveled in a 1927 review, Hughes added the verse form of the blues to poetry in English (a form that continues to attract the best black poets, including Michael Harper, Sherley Anne Williams, and Raymond Patterson).
One wonders, too, in his aspect as a poet, why this apparently happy, apparently shallow man defined his creativity in terms of unhappiness. "I felt
bad for the next three or four years," he would write in *The Big Sea* about the
period beginning more or less with the publication of "The Negro Speaks
of Rivers," "and those were the years when I wrote most of my poetry. (For
my best poems were all written when I felt the worst. When I was happy, I
didn't write anything)."

Hughes actively promoted the image of geniality to which I have al-
luded. Wanting and needing to be loved, he scrubbed and polished his per-
sonality until there was no abrasive side, no jagged edge that might wound
another human being. Publicly and privately, his manner belied the commonly held belief that creativity and madness are allied, that neuroses and a
degree of malevolence are the fair price of art. His autobiographies, *The Big
Sea* (1940) and *I Wonder As I Wander* (1956), made no enemies; to many
readers, Hughes's mastery of that form consists in his ability to cross its chill
deep by paddling nonchalantly on its surface. And yet in two places, no doubt
deliberately, Hughes allows the reader a glimpse of inner turmoil. Both appear in the earlier book, *The Big Sea*. Both involve personal and emotional
conflicts so intense that they led to physical illness. Because of their extreme
rarity, as well as their strategic location in the context of his creativity, these
passages deserve close scrutiny if we hope to glimpse the roots of Hughes's
originality as a poet.

The first of these two illnesses took place in the summer of 1919, when
Hughes (at seventeen) saw his father for the first time in a dozen years. In
1903, James Hughes had gone to Mexico, where he would become a pros-
perous property owner. In a lonely, impoverished, passed-around childhood
in the Midwest, his son had fantasized about the man "as a kind of strong,
bronze cowboy, in a big Mexican hat, going back and forth from his business in the city to his ranch in the mountains, free—in a land where there
were no white folks to draw the color line, and no tenements with rent always due—just mountains and cacti: Mexico!" Elated to be invited suddenly to Mexico in 1919 at the end of his junior year in high school,
Langston left the United States with high hopes for his visit.

The summer was a disaster. James Hughes proved to be an unfeeling,
domineering, and materialistic man, scornful of Indians and blacks (he was
himself black) and the poor in general, and contemptuous of his son's gentler
pace and artistic temperament. One day, Langston could take no more: "Suddenly my stomach began to turn over and over. And I could not swallow

another mouthful. Waves of heat engulfed me. My eyes burned. My body shook. I wanted more than anything on earth to hit my father, but instead I got up from the table and went back to bed. The bed went round and round and the room turned dark. Anger clotted in every vein, and my tongue tasted like dry blood." But the boy, ill for a long time, never confessed the true cause of his affliction. Having been moved to Mexico City, he declined to help his doctors: "I never told them . . . that I was sick because I hated my father." He recovered only when it was time to return to the United States.

Hughes's second major illness came eleven years later. By this time he had finished high school, returned to Mexico to live with his father for a year, attended Columbia University for one year (supported grudgingly by James Hughes), dropped out of school, and served as a messman on voyages to Africa and to Europe, where he spent several months in 1924 as a dishwasher. All the while, however, Hughes was publishing poetry in a variety of places, especially in important black journals. This activity culminated in books of verse published in 1926 (*The Weary Blues*) and 1927 (*Fine Clothes to the Jew*) that established him, with Countee Cullen, as one of two major black poets of the decade. In 1929, he graduated after three and a half years at black Lincoln University, Pennsylvania. In 1930, Hughes published his first novel, *Not Without Laughter*.

This book had been virtually dragged out of him by his patron of the preceding three years, "Godmother" (as she wished to be called), an old, white, very generous but eccentric woman who ruled Hughes with a benevolent despotism inspired by her volatile beliefs in African spirituality, folk culture, mental telepathy, and the potential of his genius. But the result of her largesse was a paradox: the more comfortable he grew, the less Hughes was inclined to create. Estranged by his apparent languor, his patron finally seized on an episode of conflict to banish him once and for all. Hughes was devastated. Surviving drafts of his letters to "Godmother" reveal him deep in self-abasement before a woman with whom he was clearly in love. Ten years later, he confessed in *The Big Sea:* "I cannot write here about that last half-hour in the big bright drawing-room high above Park Avenue . . . because when I think about it, even now, something happens in the pit of my stomach that makes me ill. That beautiful room . . . suddenly became like a trap closing in, faster and faster, the room darker and darker, until the light went out with a sudden crash in the dark, and everything became like . . . that morning in Mexico when I suddenly hated my father.

"I was violently and physically ill, with my stomach turning over and over. . . . And there was no rationalizing anything. I couldn't." For several months, according to my research (Hughes erroneously presents a far briefer time frame in *The Big Sea*), he waited in excruciating hope for a reconciliation.

As in Mexico, he wasted time and money on doctors without revealing to them the source of his chronic illness (which one very ingenious Harlem physician diagnosed as a Japanese tapeworm). Rather than break his silence, Hughes even agreed to have his tonsils removed. Gradually it became clear that reconciliation was impossible. Winning a prize of four hundred dollars for his novel, Hughes fled to seclusion in hot, remote Haiti. When his money ran out some months later, he returned home, healed at last but badly scarred.

Although they occurred more than a decade apart, the two illnesses were similar. Both showed a normally placid Hughes driven into deep rage by an opponent, a rage which he was unable to ventilate because the easy expression of personal anger and indignation was anathema to him. In both cases, he developed physical symptoms of hyperventilation and, eventually, anemia. More importantly, both were triggered in a period of relatively low poetic creativity (as when he was still a juvenile poet) or outright poetic inactivity (as with his patron). In each instance, Hughes had become satisfied with this low creativity or inactivity. At both times, a certain powerful figure, first his father, then "Godmother," had opposed his right to be content. His father had opposed any poetic activity at all; "Godmother" had opposed his right to enjoy the poetical state without true poetical action, or writing. In other words, a powerful will presented itself in forceful opposition to what was, in one sense, a vacuum of expressive will on Hughes's part. (Needless to say, the *apparent* absence of will in an individual can easily be a token of the presence of a very powerful will.) The result on both occasions, which was extraordinary, was first Hughes's endurance of, then his violent rebellion against, a force of will that challenged his deepest vision of the poetic life.

I use the term "will" knowing that to many people it is an obsolete concept, in spite of the revival of interest in Otto Rank, or continuing critiques of Freud's use of the term as, for example, Harold Bloom's excellent essay "Freud's Concepts of Defense and the Poetic Will." But I am referring here mainly, though not exclusively, to the will as a function of consciousness, as in the case of "Godmother's" will, or that of Hughes's father, or—far less demonstrably—Hughes's own volition. And what do I mean by Hughes's "vision of the poetic life"? I refer to what one might call unshaped or amorphous poetic consciousness, poetry not concretized or written down, but the crucial element (when combined with poetic "material") out of which written or oral poetry is made. In an old-fashioned but still significant way, the poet Richard Eberhart has written of "Will and Psyche in Poetry" (in Don Cameron Allen's *The Moment of Poetry*, 1962). Poems of the will value the body, activity, struggle, and the things of this world; poems of the psyche endorse spirit, "an uncontaminated grace," and the "elusive, passive, imaginative quality" of the world beyond this world. A poem of will, such as Marvell's "To His Coy Mistress," might involve a man calling a woman to bed; for an exemplary poem of psyche, Eberhart chose Poe's "To Helen," where desire leads directly away from sexuality toward spirit.

The notorious placidity of surface in Hughes, as I see it, bespeaks the extent to which he was a poet who preferred his poems unwritten—a poet, like his great mentor Walt Whitman, who saw his life itself as a poem greater than any poem he could possibly write. Hughes's greatest poetical instinct was to preserve his unformed or dormant poetic consciousness as the highest form of poetry. Such an instinct may suggest infantilism; one remembers Freud's unfortunate words about the link between creative writing and daydreaming. Infantilism would be wrong as an explanation. But, in Hughes's case, I suspect, the instinct had something to do with the youthfulness of the self he clearly regarded as his authentic, or most cherished self. Placidity of surface, anxiety to please and to be loved, apparent asexuality (the most consistent conclusion—rather than that of homosexuality, for which there is no evidence—about his libido among people who knew him well), and the compulsion against concretized or written poetry reflect a sense of self as prepubescent, or apubescent; in other words, a sense of self as an eternal child. At some level, Hughes saw himself ideally as a child—a dreamy genius child, a perfect child, a princely child, a loving child, even a mothering and maternal child—but first and foremost as a child (almost never is he the destructively rebellious child, in spite of his radical poetry).

It must be stressed that such a sense of self, although it modulates art (as does every other factor of comparable importance), is by no means an inherent handicap to a creative person. In any event, Hughes teetered between a sense of confidence (a sense of being loved by a particular person to whom he was emotionally mortgaged) and a rival, harrowing sense, born in his own childhood, of abandonment and despair. The latter was closer to the origins of his poetry. Release Hughes as an artist from the stabilizing social context and he flies almost immediately toward themes of nihilism and death. For example, take his poem "Border Line":

I used to wonder
About living and dying—
I think the difference lies
Between tears and crying.

I used to wonder
About here and there—
I think the distance
Is nowhere.

Or "Genius Child":

> *. . . Nobody loves a genius child.*
>
> Can you love an eagle,
> Tame or wild?
>
> Wild or tame,
> Can you love a monster
> Of frightening name?
>
> *Nobody loves a genius child.*
>
> *Kill him*—and let his soul run wild!

Or "End":

> There are
> No clocks on the wall,
> And no time,
> No shadows that move
> From dawn to dusk
> Across the floor.
>
> There is neither light
> Nor dark
> Outside the door.
>
> *There is no door!*

In Hughes's writing, there is precious little middle ground between such verse and that for which he is far better known (and deservedly so), the poems steeped in race and other social concerns. Nature as flora and fauna bored the man who preferred Harlem in hot summer to the cool New England woods, as he once joked, because "I prefer wild people to wild animals." Hughes understood wherein his salvation rested.

This bleakness, almost always ignored in critical treatments of Hughes, evolved out of the saturation of his dormant poetical consciousness by the powerful will toward death stimulated in him by his loneliness as a child. But Hughes did not surrender passively to the force of his father and "Godmother" when they turned against him. These attacks, in fact, elicited in him a massive retaliatory display of willfulness, at first (while he was ill) as uncontrolled and uncontrollable as the right to the passive poetic consciousness it defended. The invocation of will in such massive degree could easily have remained as toxic as it was while he was sick with his silent rage. Only the modification of will, a compromise between passive poetic consciousness and the purposefulness needed to defend that consciousness, could prevent the consummation of poetry (amorphous or concrete) by rage. And only an appeal to a third force that was neither Hughes nor his enemy could allow him to fashion a balance between will and his unformed poetical consciousness.

Both in the experience with his father in Mexico and in the struggle with "Godmother," the third force was represented by the black race. Hughes's attitude to the black masses is too complicated to detail here. But my argument depends on the crucial understanding that Hughes was virtually unique among major black writers not so much because of the considerable depth of his love of black people, but because of *the depth of his psychological dependence on them.* Hughes became dependent because of a relatively complicated set of circumstances in his youth, when he was reared by his poor but very proud grandmother, the aged, wrinkled, and laconic Mary Langston, whose first husband had died at Harpers Ferry with John Brown. But Mary Langston's zeal to defend the rights of her race was offset for her grandson by her personal remoteness both from him and the race, and by the severity of her pride—a pride compounded by her very light skin, her Indian rather than predominantly African features, her Oberlin education, and her high-toned religion, which all kept her distant from the black masses. She did not attend black churches, did not sing black spirituals (much less the blues); she spoke in a clipped manner, rather than a folksy drawl, and she detested popular culture—as Hughes spelled out partially in *The Big Sea,* but more completely in an unpublished portrait prepared in 1943.

What Mary Langston offered in the abstract, however, was made wonderfully concrete to young Hughes by two persons with whom he lived from time to time (when his grandmother was forced to rent out her house, and after she died) and whom he described in an Arcadian paragraph in *The Big Sea*—"Uncle" and "Auntie" Reed. "Uncle" James Reed, who dug ditches for the city, smoked his pipe and stayed home on Sundays. "Auntie" Reed (later Mrs. Mary J. Reed Campbell) took Langston to St. Luke's A.M.E. church (a church apparently not good enough for his grandmother) and taught the Sunday School there in which the boy was the brightest star. Through the childless Reeds, who clearly adored the boy, he learned how to love the race, its church ways and folk ways, and its dreams and aspirations, of which the handsome, scrubbed, light brown boy, the grandson of "Colonel" Charles Langston (whose brother John Mercer Langston had served in the U.S. Congress and as an ambassador of the U.S.) was the shining embodiment. And it was a lie he told to the Reeds (that Jesus had come to Hughes at a revival meeting, after "Auntie" Reed had prayed that this would happen) that led to the major trauma of his childhood, as related in *The Big Sea*—a long weeping into the night (the second to last time he cried, Hughes wrote) because he had waited for Jesus, who had never come, then had lied to the people who loved him most. In *The Big Sea* Hughes would admit to hating his father; he would partly ridicule his mother; he would admit that he did not cry when his grandmother died. The Reeds, however, were different: "For me, there have never been any better people in the world. I loved them very much."

In his bitter struggles with his father and "Godmother," Hughes turned to the black race for direction. But one needs to remember that this appeal in itself hardly gave Hughes distinction as a poet; what made Hughes distinct was the highly original manner in which he internalized the Afro-American racial dilemma and expressed it in poems such as "When Sue Wears Red," "The Negro Speaks of Rivers," "Mother to Son," "Dream Variations," and "The Weary Blues," poems of Hughes's young manhood on which his career would rest. Of these, the most important was "The Negro Speaks of Rivers."

> I've known rivers.
> I've known rivers ancient as the world and older
>   than the flow of human blood in human veins.
>
> My soul has grown deep like the rivers.
>
> I bathed in the Euphrates when dawns were young.
> I built my hut near the Congo and it lulled me to sleep.
> I looked upon the Nile and raised the pyramids above it.
> I heard the singing of the Mississippi when Abe Lincoln
>   went down to New Orleans, and I've seen its muddy
>   bosom turn all golden in the sunset.
>
> I've known rivers:
> Ancient, dusky rivers.
>
> My soul has grown deep like the rivers.

Here, the persona moves steadily from dimly starred personal memory ("I've known rivers") toward a rendezvous with modern history (Lincoln going down the Mississippi and seeing the horror of slavery that, according to legend, would make him one day free the slaves). The death wish, benign but suffusing, of its images of rivers older than human blood, of souls grown as deep as these rivers, gives way steadily to an altering, ennobling vision whose final effect gleams in the evocation of the Mississippi's "muddy bosom" turning at last "all golden in the sunset." Personal anguish has been alchemized by the poet into a gracious meditation on his race, whose despised ("muddy") culture and history, irradiated by the poet's vision, changes within the poem from mud into gold. This is a classic example of the essential process of creativity in Hughes.

The poem came to him, according to Hughes (accurately, it seems clear) about ten months after his Mexican illness, when he was riding a train from Cleveland to Mexico to rejoin his father. The time was sundown, the place the Mississippi outside St. Louis. "All day on the train I had been thinking of my father," he would write in *The Big Sea*. "Now it was just sunset and we crossed the Mississippi, slowly, over a long bridge. I looked out of the window of the Pullman at the great muddy river flowing down toward the heart of the South, and I began to think what that river, the old Mississippi, had meant to Negroes in the past—how to be sold down the river was the worst fate that could overtake a slave in bondage. Then I remembered reading how Abraham Lincoln had made a trip down the Mississippi on a raft, and how he had seen slavery at its worst, and had decided within himself that it should be removed from American life. Then I began to think of other rivers in our past—the Congo, and the Niger, and the Nile in Africa—and the thought came to me: 'I've known rivers,' and I put it down on the back of an envelope I had in my pocket, and within the space of ten or fifteen minutes, as the train gathered speed in the dusk, I had written this poem."

Here, starting with anguish over his father, Hughes discovered the compressed ritual of passivity, challenge, turmoil, and transcendence he would probably have to re-create, doubtless in variant forms, during the great poetic trysts of his life. Even after he became a successful, published poet, the basic process remained the same, because his psychology remained largely the same even though he had become technically expert. In his second major illness, caused by his patron "Godmother," Hughes wrote poetry as he struggled for a transcendence that would be long in coming. The nature of that interim poetry is telling. When he sent some poems to a friend for a little book to be printed privately, she noticed at once that many spoke of death—"Dear lovely Death /That taketh all things under wing—/Never to kill. . . ." She called the booklet *Dear Lovely Death*. In "Afro-American Fragment," unlike in "The Negro Speaks of Rivers," Africa is seen plaintively:

> . . . Subdued and time-lost
> Are the drums—and yet
> Through some vast mist of race
> There comes this song

I do not understand,
This song of atavistic land,
Of bitter yearnings lost
Without a place—
So long,
So far away
Is Africa's
Dark face.

But when Hughes returned home, scarred but healed, after months in seclusion in Haiti, he no longer thought of loss and death. Instead, he plunged directly into the life of the black masses with a seven-month tour of the South in which he read his poetry in their churches and schools. Then he set out for the Soviet Union, where he would spend more than a year. Hughes then reached the zenith of his revolutionary ardor with poems (or verse) such as "Good Morning Revolution," "Goodbye Christ," and "Put One More 'S' in the USA."

"Good Morning Revolution," for example, and "The Negro Speaks of Rivers" are very different poems. The former is the polar opposite of the poetry of nihilism; the latter blends aspects of existential gloom with the life-affirming spirit of the black race. Together, the poems illustrate the wide range of possibility in the mixture of will and passivity which characterizes Hughes's art (although one can argue that "Good Morning Revolution"— by far the lesser poem—marks an overreaction of will, and thus is not truly representative of Hughes's poetic temperament in that it contains no element of passivity). But the creative process has remained the same. The right to amorphous poetic consciousness is challenged. The will is aroused in defense of that consciousness. Illness (an extreme version of Wallace Stevens' "blessed rage for order"?) marks the struggle of will against opposing will. The long-endured illness, in silence, gradually allows the mutual fertilization of will and poetic consciousness that is needed for concrete art. Illness ends when that ratio is achieved or perceived, and writing begins. Creativity, in Keats's term, has created itself. A poet, or a poem, is born.

To some extent, this process is nothing more than Wordsworth's definition of poetry as the final recollection "in tranquility" (a phrase often underplayed or even ignored in quoting Wordsworth's definition) of emotion that had once spontaneously overflowed. What is different, of course, is that Wordsworth (and Keats and Stevens) did not have to contend with race as a factor in his creativity. For many writers, perhaps even most, race is a distracting, demoralizing force. Hughes's genius, or his good fortune, consisted in his ability to accommodate race harmoniously within the scheme of creativity common to all major poets, and to turn it from an anomaly into an intimate advantage.

STEVEN C. TRACY

"Midnight Ruffles of Cat-Gut Lace": The Boogie Poems of Langston Hughes
(1988)

The influence of the blues tradition on Langston Hughes' poetry is by now an oft-discussed and readily accepted fact, although the depth and breadth of his employment of the tradition has not often been discussed with a similar depth and breadth. A close examination of a related sequence of Hughes' blues poems offers the opportunity to explore his fusion of oral and written traditions and to examine his tremendous skills as a literary-jazz improviser. That is not to suggest that Hughes' poems are spontaneous creations. Improvisation is normally thought of as a spontaneous act, but the jazz or blues musician's improvisations are in fact bounded by several things: the musician's "vocabulary"—style, patterns, techniques, and riffs; the accepted conventions of the specific genre (even if those conventions are deliberately violated, they are, in a large sense, at work); and the boundaries of the individual piece being performed. For example, boogie-woogie pianist Pete Johnson, in his 1947 version of "Swanee River Boogie," performs the melody of the song to a boogie-woogie beat, thereafter improvising solos built around the song's chord changes, the boogie-woogie beat, and variations on the melody of the piece, combined with his arsenal of boogie-woogie riffs and performed in his inimitable style.[1] Hughes, in his 1951 collection, *Montage of a Dream Deferred,* generated a set or sequence of six "boogie" poems—"Dream Boogie," "Easy Boogie," "Boogie 1 a.m.," "Lady's Boogie," "Nightmare Boogie," and "Dream Boogie: Variation"—that have in common much more than the "boogie" of the titles. The poems comprise an intricate series of interwoven "improvisations" over a set boogie-woogie rhythm, with Hughes modulating and modifying rhythm, words, imagery, moods, and themes, and constructing a complex interrelationship between

---

[1] Pete Johnson, "Swanee River Boogie," *Boogie Woogie Trio,* Storyville SLP 4006, 1976.

music, the musical instrument, the performance, and a set of attitudes exemplified by them.

Structurally, Hughes' six boogie poems share the exciting, rushing rhythms of boogie-woogie: Hughes at work on his poems, pounding out rhythms on his typewriter keyboard. Briefly, boogie-woogie is a form of Afro-American music, normally performed on the piano, that emerged as a recognizable genre in the 1920s. As blues researcher Karl Gert zur Heide points out, "the theme of boogie is the blues, some features derive from ragtime, and the rhythmic interplay of both hands can be traced back to African roots."[2] In boogie-woogie, the improvisations executed by the pianist's right hand on the treble keys of the piano are set off against the ostinato or repeated phrases of the left hand on the bass keys. Characteristically boogie-woogie follows the twelve-bar blues chord change pattern—in the key of C, CFC GFC—employing a repeated bass pattern recognizable most often for its eight beats to the bar and performed at a medium-to-fast tempo that builds an explosive drive and swing appropriate to the dance step after which it was named. Besides identifying a dance step and a type of music, however, the term "boogie" functions in other contexts: to boogie is to raise a ruckus or act wildly or uninhibitedly; it also has sexual connotations:

> I'm gonna pull off my pants and keep on my shirt,
> I'm gonna get so low you think I'm in the dirt.
> I'm gonna pitch a boogie-woogie,
> Gonna boogie-woogie all night long.[3]

In this tune, singer Big Bill Broonzy has taken a boogie-woogie beat suitable for dancing and provided both the "wild acting" and sexual connotations that go with it. In the tradition, the word carried these connotations, and typically Hughes tried to capture the ambience of the tradition.

Hughes demonstrated his knowledge of boogie-woogie in *The First Book of Jazz,* in which he and his coauthors identified among the outstanding exponents of boogie-woogie "Pinetop" Smith, Jimmy Yancy, Meade Lux Lewis, Albert Ammons, and Pete Johnson—all important and generally recognized masters.[4] It was the spirited, exuberant, danceable, and often

---

[2] Karl Gert zur Heide, *Deep South Piano* (London: Studio Vista, 1970), p. 11.

[3] Big Bill Broonzy, "Let's Reel and Rock," Melotone, 7-06-64, 1936, 78 R.P.M. recording.

[4] Langston Hughes, Cliff Roberts, and David Martin, *The First Book of Jazz* (New York: Franklin Watts, Inc., 1955).

rhythmically complex and intricate music of performers like those men that provided the basis for Hughes' boogie poem rhythms and the connotations of the word and the tradition that he tried to capture in his poems.

Hughes obviously wanted us to hear the boogie rhythms in these poems: the first four poems in the boogie sequence ("Dream," "Easy," "1 a.m.," and "Lady's") are very "aural"; the words "hear" and "heard" are employed repeatedly, both in a question—

> Ain't you heard
> The boogie-woogie rumble
> Of a dream deferred?[5]

and an assertion—

> I know you've heard
> The boogie-woogie rumble
> Of a dream deferred. ("Boogie 1 a.m.," p. 250)

The incessant rhythm and rumbling of boogie-woogie becomes in the poems symbolic of the dream he had delineated in his earlier poem "Dream Variations":

> To fling my arms wide
> In some place of the sun,
> To whirl and to dance
> Till the white day is done.
> Then rest at cool evening
> Beneath a tall tree
> While night comes on gently,
>   Dark like me—
> That is my dream! ("Dream Variations," p. 14)

Hughes is trying to get black people to recognize that the deferment of that dream is a large part of their lives, both by questioning and by asserting the "obvious." If they hadn't heard that boogie-woogie rumble, they could certainly hear it in the rhythms of Hughes' poems; for example, if one were to treat "Dream Boogie," the first poem of the sequence and therefore a prototype for the other poems in the sequence, as if it were a lyric to be sung to boogie-woogie music, and identify the beats and chord changes as they relate to the words, the annotation would look as follows:

---

[5] Langston Hughes, *Selected Poems* (New York: Vintage Books, 1974), p. 221. All further references to Hughes' poems will be followed in the text by page numbers from this work.

      C

    1 2 34 567 8

Good morning, daddy!

1 2 34 5 6 7

Ain't you heard

  8   12   34   56

The boogie-woogie rumble

 7 8 12   34 56   7 8

Of a dream deferred?

F

1234 567

Listen closely:

  8   12   34   5 6 7 8

You'll hear their feet

   C

  1 2 3 4   5 6 7 8

Beating out and beating out a—
You think
It's a happy beat?

G

1 2 3 4 5 67 8

Listen to it closely:

F

1 2 3 4 5 6 78

Ain't you heard

   C

  1   2   3 4 5 6 7 8

Something underneath like a—

What did I say?
Sure,
I'm happy!
Take it away!

Hey pop!
Re-bop!
Mop!

Y-e-a-h! ("Dream Boogie," p. 221)

What Hughes has done is create a twelve-line, twelve-bar boogie-woogie poem, annexing an exclamatory "tag" ending like those occasionally employed in music. Here, though, Hughes has manipulated the form and rhythm: stanzas two and three are jarred by the dramatic insertion of disturbing questions that achieve their impact by rewording the line we would expect in the normal rhythm and progression of thoughts into a question. Thus, in stanza two, "Beating out and beating out a happy beat" becomes:

Beating out and beating out—

You think
It's a happy beat?

Just as Hughes shifts to the interrogative and separates those questions from their normal stanzaic group, he just as surely upsets the boogie-woogie rhythm, eventually violating even the rhyming pattern in stanza three. This is significant because stanza three draws on the first two stanzas for a repetition of important lines: "Listen closely" of stanza two becomes "Listen to it closely" (Hughes employs a common characteristic of blues lyrics, building slightly modulated lines around loose formulaic patterns) in stanza three, while "Ain't you heard" of stanza one is lifted verbatim. Stanza three, however, becomes deliberately vague—"Something underneath"—in order to force the audience to answer the subsequent question, "What did I say?" By upsetting the rhythm and asking the questions, Hughes highlights the disparity between the rumbling seriousness of the deferred dream and the superficial happiness of the beat or performance. To this masterful maneuvering of the idiom Hughes annexes the "tag" ending—in jazz and blues a four-bar section appended to the end of a tune that repeats a phrase, offers a final comment, or indicates that the performance is about to end—often for those dancing to the performance. Hughes' seven-line ending contrasts once again the happiness of the words / music performance with the underlying problem. In light of the dramatic irony with which Hughes dealt with the subject earlier, this return to the facade of carefree happiness adds psychological complexity to the poem. Hughes felt that blacks needed to recognize the reality of deferred dreams, as he has forced in stanza three, but in stanza four he emphasizes the need to retain the spirit of cultural expression and the usefulness of the elaborate role-playing that provided blacks with the opportunity for advances, while whites concentrate on the superficial happy roles that blacks played.

The boogie rhythms extend to other poems in the sequence, although the twelve-bar progression is not necessarily present in any of them. "Easy Boogie," "Nightmare Boogie," and "Dream Boogie: Variation" could theoretically fit into the twelve-bar pattern annotated with the variations above. One indication that they may not have been intended to fit into the twelve-bar pattern is the presence, in "Easy Boogie," of the line "Riffs, smears, breaks" between stanzas two and three, which seems to indicate an instrumental break that would not be characteristic in a standard twelve-bar blues—the breaks would come between the twelve-bar verses. This underscores the importance of "hearing" the boogie-woogie rhythm and spirit of the performance as opposed to following a predetermined structure. "Lady's Boogie" and "Boogie 1 a.m." reemphasize the distinction, each of them eight-line poems (with an additional mock-jive exclamation in the former) in boogie rhythm. These poems, then, are tied together by the rhythm and spirit of boogie-woogie—a rhythm and spirit that Hughes clearly intended for us to hear.

The poems, of course, have other features in common besides boogie-woogie rhythm. The first four poems in the sequence all employ black jive slang: in "Dream Boogie" he uses "Daddy!" and "Hey pop! Re-bop! Mop! Y-e-a-h!"; in "Easy Boogie" he uses "Hey, Lawdy Mama!"; in "'Boogie 1 a.m." he uses "Daddy!"; and in "Lady's Boogie" he employs the phrase "Be-Bach!" Coupled with the boogie rhythms this plying of black speech demonstrates the influence of oral culture on Hughes' work, giving the distinctively black flavor to the poems necessary to suggest encoded messages appropriate to a segregated group of people. Music critic John McDonough has pointed out the usefulness of slang code words:

> There is a fraternal link that always seems to bond together those who would challenge or otherwise separate themselves from the mainstream of social custom. Sometimes the trappings and devices of such brotherhood are enjoyed for their own sake—a sort of college game without substance. But more commonly, they have a very specific and necessary function. In a hostile and crowded world, such devices identify each member to the other. It may be a handshake, a secret word or phrase, gesture or symbol. In short, a lexicon of code words that separate the true believers from the indifferent or unfriendly.[6]

Hughes doesn't employ code words that whites are unlikely to understand, but the words are readily identifiable with black culture, and by doing so he intimates that his message is directed at blacks and, to a great measure, originates with them.

This slang also helps call attention to the similarities and contrasts of the poems. Both "Dream Boogie" and "Boogie 1 a.m.," for example, are narrated

---

[6] John McDonoough, Jacket Notes, *Tea Pad Songs, Vol. 2,* Stash Records ST-104, n.d.

by women, as indicated by the address "Daddy." This address, along with "Papa," is common in the blues songs of females and in black culture in general, but the term of address would not be used by a male; "Daddy-o" would be used, but not simply "Daddy." This use of a female speaker, which is also prevalent in Hughes' blues poems, is important in that it indicates that the ideas are not necessarily identifiable with a single viewpoint: that of the black male Hughes. The suggestion is that the problems of blacks connected with deferred dreams is not simply an intricate artistic stance of the author, but the representative stance of sensitive blacks, both male and female, who, especially in terms of the sexual theme of the poems, will be creating future generations.

"Dream Boogie" is a poem of beginnings: besides being the first poem of the sequence, it is the poem that greets at the beginning of the day and poses the nagging and disconcerting questions dealt with repeatedly in the other poems. It is appropriate that this is the first poem in the sequence, since upon awakening one would have the best chance of recalling dreams, and awakening from the fantasy/dream world to reality would accentuate the disparity between those two worlds. In "Dream Boogie" the speaker asks questions, in contrast to "Boogie 1 a.m.," a poem of conclusion that addresses the listener at day's end—"Good evening, Daddy"—and asserts that the listener is aware of the rumblings of the dream deferred, presumable after day-long contact with the white-controlled world.

Similarly, "Easy Boogie," the second poem of the sequence, and "Lady's Boogie," the fourth, are related. In contrast to "Dream Boogie," in "Easy Boogie" a man addresses a woman—"Hey, Lawdy Mama!" The speaker associates the recognition of the steady beat of the dream deferred with the vitality of the sexual act:

> Hey, Lawdy Mama!
> Do you hear what I said?
> Easy like I rock it
> In my bed! ("Easy Boogie," pp. 229–30)

This sexual vitality, implicit in the word "boogie," as already pointed out, is also linked with the soul's aspirations through the repetition of sentence construction:

> Down in the bass
> That easy roll
> Rolling like I like it
> In my soul.

The souls' dreams are seen as vital, lively, and life-giving. Thus through the repetition of phrases and structures, Hughes expands the importance of his words beyond their initial or superficial meanings.

"Lady's Boogie" exposes the superficial concerns of a posturing "lady" who

> ain't got boogie-woogie
> On her mind. ("Lady's Boogie," p. 251)

Viewed in comparison to "Easy Boogie," the sexual connotation is at work here, suggesting a sexually ineffectual or inhibited person and connecting that to the inability to hear the beat of the dream deferred. Hughes suggests that the "Lady" has not listened, and could be successful if she did:

> But if she was to listen
> I bet she'd hear
> Way up in the treble
> The tingle of a tear.

However, the final exclamation ("Be-Bach!") suggests that her pretense makes a mockery of her own people's language in combining the phrase be-bop with the classical composer from another culture, mocking the pretension of her position and making it seem ludicrous.

"Easy Boogie" and "Lady's Boogie" also begin to deal with the relationships between the performer/creator, his instrument, and his creation, as they relate to the underlying desires and feelings of blacks. Although the "boogie-woogie rumble of a dream deferred" played "underneath" on the bass keys of a piano had already been introduced in "Dream Boogie," "Easy Boogie" further connects the bass rumble with something "down," something "underneath," something sexual, something elemental. It is the walking bass of solidarity:

> Down in the bass
> That steady beat
> Walking, walking, walking
> Like marching feet. ("Easy Boogie," pp. 229–30)

This solidarity is connected, through repetition and parallel sentence structure, with the feeling of the soul:

> Down in the bass
> that steady roll
> Rolling like I like it
> In my soul.

Conversely, "Lady's Boogie" deals with the speaker's attitude toward a woman who has allowed the pretensions of "society" to interfere with her realizations about the problems of her people. This woman's mind is linked to the notes played in the treble on the piano:

> See that lady
> Dressed so fine
> She ain't got boogie-woogie
> On her mind—
>
> But if she was to listen
> I bet she'd hear
> Way up in the treble
> The tingle of a tear. ("Lady's Boogie," p. 251)

Once again the lines relate through their parallel structures: the lady whose pretensions prevent her from "hearing," being aware; who concentrates on appearances rather than sounds, messages; who doesn't listen to the agent that would "enlighten" her, the treble improvisations; whose mind refuses her emotional involvement with the boogie-woogie message. Hughes is, in effect, replicating the amazing dexterity and remarkable rhythmic diversity of the boogie-woogie pianist: he is combining the rumbling, infectious bass beat and rhythm with treble variations and improvisations, relating the former to the "soul" and action, and the latter to the mind and thought of the "movement" to foster awareness of the problems of black people in terms of the deferred dream. The staccato alliteration is particularly effective in "Lady's Boogie," "Boogie 1 a.m." ("trilling the treble"), and "Dream Boogie: Variation" ("tinkling treble"), particularly when picked out over the momentum of the rolling bass.

These treble and bass patterns are used to introduce and indeed are a part of the compelling unifying image of the poems:

> Trilling the treble
> And twining the bass
> Into midnight ruffles
> of cat-gut lace. ("Boogie 1 a.m.," p. 250)

Here the right-hand treble notes and the left-hand bass notes are united in performance, just as the mind and soul or thought and feeling of blacks are meant to be united in a common cause: the recognition of the dream deferred and the organization into a unified front to confront the problems of blacks in America. Hughes did not want to overemphasize the bass/sex/soul of the second poem of the sequence, "Easy Boogie"; neither did he want to concentrate exclusively on the treble/inhibitions/mind of the fourth poem, "Lady's Boogie." It was the poem in between, "Boogie 1 a.m.," that presented the "unified sensibility" for which Hughes aimed and that combined the bass and treble into a single compelling image.

The image itself at once suggests several things: ruffles and lace both suggest the delicate trimming of clothing; however, to be ruffled is to become disturbed, and to ruffle is to cause disturbances, as in water; the lace becomes something to hold things together in light of the "cat-gut" prefix. All these combine to suggest a decorative appearance tied to an underlying disquietedness. The "midnight" of "midnight ruffles" identifies the revelation as a black one and places the revelation at nighttime—the time of dreams and nightmares.

A variation of the image returns in "Nightmare Boogie," which follows "Lady's Boogie" and, with "Dream Boogie: Variation," helps emphasize the dream theme at the end of the sequence. "Nightmare Boogie" deals with the collective loss of black identity:

> I had a dream
> and I could see
> a million faces
> black as me!
>
> A nightmare dream:
> *Quicker than light*
> *All them faces*
> *Turned dead white!* ("Nightmare Boogie," p. 258)

This sentiment is a magnification of the problem recognized in "Lady's Boogie," where the "lady" has lost the ability to hear and understand cultural messages. In "Nightmare" Hughes identifies the instantaneous loss of black identity as a phenomenon that occurred more quickly than it could be recognized, more quickly than it could be exposed, thus stressing the urgency of black identity, pride, and unity. What is important here is that the first four lines have a direct parallel relationship to lines five through eight: the dream of line one is the nightmare of line five; the seeing of line two is the revelation of line six; the faces of lines three and seven and the colors of lines four and eight define whether the event was a dream or a nightmare. At the climax of the metamorphosis from black to white, from dream to nightmare, Hughes eschews a smooth transition, generating a "whirling" midnight incantation, as if awakening to a real solution:

> Boogie-woogie,
> Rolling bass,
> Whirling treble
> Of cat-gut lace. ("Nightmare Boogie," p. 258)

This variation on the lines of "Boogie 1 a.m." labels the dream deferred as a nightmare that leads to a racial identity, resolvable only by hearing and understanding the "message" of boogie-woogie.

In contrast to the nightmare of the dream deferred, the black pride / identity "movement," the marching, walking feet of "Dream Boogie" and "Easy Boogie," is a whirling awakening to a new dream, which forms a very natural sequence to "Dream Boogie: Variation"—the final poem of the entire sequence—and a counterpoint to "Dream Boogie," the first. Whereas "Dream Boogie" is an upbeat, urgent poem, "Variation" is much more sad and subdued: the portrait of the boogie-woogie pianist, performing his music, his piano screaming for him under his lone stomping feet, his eyes misting at the prospect of having missed his chance at freedom. Here, however, the "midnight ruffles of / cat-gut lace" of the "Boogie 1 a.m." quatrain, and the "Whirling treble / of cat-gut lace" of the "Nightmare Boogie" quatrain become "High noon teeth / In a midnight face," identifying the central idea and image of the poems with the actual facial features and identity of the performer, the creator, the one closest to the music itself. Hughes is emphasizing here how easy it is for an individual to fail to recognize the dream deferred, the nightmare as it relates to the individual himself. The final image is not the jive-talking, energetic persona of "Dream Boogie"; it is the embodiment of the boogie-woogie tradition, alone and too late, playing the wistful boogie of freedom deferred.

By varying and manipulating the rhythm, words, imagery, moods, and themes of these poems, Hughes has illuminated the issue of the dream deferred from different emotional perspectives. By employing folk culture so well, he in effect gives his poems traditional authority, makes them unadulteratedly black, and establishes a continuity that makes them seem to express the ideas of the people for the people.

Karen Jackson Ford

Do Right to Write Right:
Langston Hughes's Aesthetics
of Simplicity
(1992)

The one thing most readers of twentieth-century American poetry can say about Langston Hughes is that he has known rivers. "The Negro Speaks of Rivers" has become memorable for its lofty, oratorical tone, mythic scope, and powerful rhythmic repetitions:

I've known rivers:
I've known rivers ancient as the world and older than
the flow of human blood in human veins.

(1656)

But however beautiful its cadences, the poem is remembered primarily because it is Hughes's most frequently anthologized work. The fact is, "The
Negro Speaks of Rivers" is one of Hughes's most uncharacteristic poems,
and yet it has defined his reputation, along with a small but constant selection of other poems included in anthologies. "A Negro Speaks of Rivers,"
"A House in Taos," "The Weary Blues," "Montage of a Dream Deferred,"
"Theme for English B," "Refugee in America," and "I, Too"—these poems
invariably comprise his anthology repertoire despite the fact that none of
them typifies his writing. What makes these poems atypical is exactly what
makes them appealing and intelligible to the scholars who edit anthologies—their complexity. True, anthologies produced in the current market,
which is hospitable to the African-American tradition and to canon reform,
now include a brief selection of poems in black folk forms. But even though
Hughes has fared better in anthologies than most African-American writers, only a small and predictable segment of his poetry has been preserved.
A look back through the original volumes of poetry, and even through the
severely redrawn *Selected Poems,* reveals a wealth of simpler poems we ought
to be reading.[1]

Admittedly, an account of Hughes's poetic simplicity requires some
qualification. Most obvious is the fact that he wrote poems that are not
simple. "A Negro Speaks of Rivers" is oracular; "The Weary Blues" concludes enigmatically; "A House in Taos" is classically modernist in both its
fragmented form and its decadent sensibility. Even more to the point, many
of the poems that have been deemed simple are only ironically so. "The
Black Christ," for example, is a little jingle that invokes monstrous cultural
complexity. Likewise, two later books, *Ask Your Mama* (1961) and *The Panther and the Lash* (1967), contain an intricate vision of American history beneath their simple surfaces.[2] Nevertheless, the overwhelming proportion of
poems in the Hughes canon consists of work in the simpler style; and even

---

[1] Easily ninety per cent of the poems in Hughes's canon are of the sort that I am describing as
simple.

[2] Jemie, Hudson, and Miller, among others, have persuasively demonstrated the intricacies of
Hughes's jazz structures in these two late books.

those poems that can yield complexities make use of simplicity in ways that ought not to be ignored. The repression of the great bulk of Hughes's poems is the result of chronic critical scorn for their simplicity. Throughout his long career, but especially after his first two volumes of poetry (readers were at first willing to assume that a youthful poet might grow to be more complex), his books received their harshest reviews for a variety of "flaws" that all originate in an aesthetics of simplicity. From his first book, *The Weary Blues* (1926), to his last one, *The Panther and the Lash* (1967), the reviews invoke a litany of faults: the poems are superficial, infantile, silly, small, unpoetic, common, jejune, iterative, and, of course, simple.[3] Even his admirers reluctantly conclude that Hughes's poetics failed. Saunders Redding flatly opposes simplicity and artfulness: "While Hughes's rejection of his own growth shows an admirable loyalty to his self-commitment as the poet of the 'simple, Negro commonfolk' . . . it does a disservice to his art" (Mullen 74). James Baldwin, who recognizes the potential of simplicity as an artistic principle, faults the poems for "tak[ing] refuge . . . in a fake simplicity in order to avoid the very difficult simplicity of the experience" (Mullen 85).

Despite a lifetime of critical disappointments, then, Hughes remained loyal to the aesthetic program he had outlined in 1926 in his decisive poetic treatise, "The Negro Artist and the Racial Mountain." There he had predicted that the common people would "give to this world its truly great Negro artist, the one who is not afraid to be himself," a poet who would explore the "great field of unused [folk] material ready for his art" and recognize that this source would provide "sufficient matter to furnish a black artist with a lifetime of creative work" (692). This is clearly a portrait of the poet Hughes would become, and he maintained his fidelity to this ideal at great cost to his literary reputation.

In what follows I will look at some of that forgotten poetry and propose a way to read it that refutes the criticism that most of Hughes's poetry is too simple for serious consideration. I will first reconstruct Hughes's conception of the poet by looking at one of his prose characters who embodies his poetics; and, second, I will turn to a reading of *Shakespeare in Harlem* (1942), a volume of poetry that typifies Hughes's aesthetic program.

In his column in the *Chicago Defender* on February 13, 1943, Hughes first introduced the prototype of the humorous and beloved fictional character Jesse B. Semple, nicknamed by his Harlem friends "Simple." For the

---

[3] Reviews in which these epithets appear are collected in Mullen.

next twenty-three years Hughes would continue to publish Simple stories both in the *Defender* and in several volumes of collected and edited pieces.[4] Hughes called Simple his "ace-boy," and it is surely not coincidental that the Simple stories span the years, the 1940s to the 1960s, when Langston Hughes needed a literary ace in the hole.[5] The success of the Simple stories was an important consolation of the writer's later years, when his poetry was reviewed with disappointment, his autobiography dismissed as "chit-chat," his plays refused on Broadway, and his fiction diminished in importance next to Richard Wright's *Native Son* (1940) and Ralph Ellison's *Invisible Man* (1952).[6]

It seems obvious, however, that in the long association with his ace-boy Hughes found more than popularity and financial success. In fact, his prefatory sketches of Simple attest to the character's importance, in the sheer number of times Hughes sets out to explain him and in the specific details these explanations provide.[7] All of them depict Simple as an African American Everyman, the authentic—even unmediated—voice of the community that engendered him. For instance, in "Who Is Simple?" Hughes emphasizes the authenticity of his creation: "[Simple's] first words came directly out of the mouth of a young man who lived just down the block from me" (*Best* vii). Here and elsewhere Hughes asserts a vital connection between the fictional character and the people he represents: "If there were not a lot of genial souls in Harlem as talkative as Simple, I would never have these tales to write down that are 'just like him'" (*Best* viii). The author's dedication to Simple is surely rooted in his conviction that Simple embodies and speaks for the very people to whom Hughes had committed himself back in the 1920s. But Hughes's affinity with Simple is more complete than this.

---

[4]   The stories are collected in five volumes, *The Best of Simple, Simple Speaks His Mind, Simple Stakes a Claim, Simple Takes a Wife,* and *Simple's Uncle Sam.* Additionally, Hughes takes Simple to the stage with *Simply Heavenly,* a comedy about Simple's marriage.

[5]   In "Who Is Simple?"—the foreword to *The Best of Simple*—Hughes concludes, "He is my ace-boy, Simple. I hope you like him, too" (viii).

[6]   For a chronicle of Hughes's disappointments during these years, see Rampersad, especially chapter 8 of the second volume "In Warm Manure: 1951 to 1953." Ellison characterized *The Big Sea* as a "chit-chat" book during an interview with Rampersad in 1983 (202).

[7]   Hughes wrote at least four explanations of Simple: "The Happy Journey of 'Simply Heavenly,'" "Simple and Me," "Who Is Simple?" and the "Character Notes" to *Simply Heavenly.*

Commentators on the Simple stories have concentrated on two points: theme, "Hughes's handling of the race issue" (Mullen 20); and genre, "the generic nature of these prose sketches" (Mullen 20).[8] It is exclusively Hughes as prose artist we have acknowledged when considering these tales. However, I will argue that the Simple stories reveal a great deal about Hughes's poetic genius as well. Casting Simple as the figure of the poet illuminates Hughes's poetic program and explains his powerful affinity with his prose creation.

Crucial in tracing Simple's significance are the "Character Notes" to the 1957 musical comedy *Simply Heavenly,* which describe Simple in terms that stress his contradictions:

> Simple is a Chaplinesque character, slight of build, awkwardly graceful, given to flights of fancy, and positive statements of opinion—stemming from a not so positive soul. He is dark with a likable smile, ordinarily dressed, except for rather flamboyant summer sports shirts. Simple tries hard to succeed, but the chips seldom fall just right. Yet he bounces like a rubber ball. He may go down, but he always bounds back up. (*Plays* 115)

The parallel to Charlie Chaplin, an icon of contradiction, is telling. Like Chaplin, whose physical appearance announces internal tensions (his hat is too small, his shoes too large, his vest too tight, his pants too loose), Simple is awkward yet graceful, ordinary yet flamboyant. And, again as with Chaplin, these external tensions reveal deeper ones; he is obstinate yet fanciful, decent yet flawed, and—perhaps most poignant for Hughes—optimistic despite failure.

Simple is a compelling figure for Hughes precisely because of these tensions. For these contraries—even the apparently internal ones—hang about Simple like a fool's motley. The fool's motley, of course, traditionally implies chaos; yet while his multicolored costume reflects the intricacies and contradictions around him, the fool himself may often be a perfect simpleton. This is also true of Hughes's character: though his appearance and even to some extent his character express contradiction, his fundamental nature is unequivocally simple. Obstinate, positivistic, and optimistic, Simple is able to register contradictions without finally resolving them and therefore has special significance for Hughes's poetic project. Hughes, after all, claims that "where life is simple, truth and reality are one" (*Big Sea* 311). Yet where in

---

[8] In his Introduction Mullen surveys the scholarship on the Simple stories; all the works he cites discuss either their racial politics or their prose structures.

America is life simple for African Americans? The "where" Hughes invokes is not a place but a state of mind. The terms of his formulation—simplicity, truth, reality—are broad and vague because they are nearly synonymous to him. If one recognizes the simple facts of life, one will be able to see the truth; if one lives by the truth, one's reality will match one's ideals. Simplicity *is* truth in Hughes's vision.

Simple is the personification of such a poetics, a philosophy of composition that resorts to simplicity, not in response to singleness or triviality, but, ironically, in response to almost unspeakable contradiction. This is why he appears surrounded by complexities—his culture, his friends, even his clothing registering the confusion of the world around him. To shift the metaphor, simpleness, in both the character and the poetry, functions as a brick wall against which complexities collide. In its artless, uncomprehending refusal to incorporate contradictions, it exacerbates them. For a poet who equates simplicity with truth, cultivating a thematics and aesthetics of simplicity is essential—poetically and politically. Simplicity resists the pernicious subtleties and complexities of integrationist thought. Further, it reveals the inadequacies of such thought. But more important, it achieves these aims by reinstating the truth.

Let me turn to some examples. In "There Ought to Be a Law," Simple tells his friend Boyd that Congress ought to pass a law "setting up a few Game Preserves for Negroes" (*Reader* 181). Having seen a short movie about wildlife preserves, where "buffaloes roams and nobody can shoot a single one of them" (181), Simple concludes that "Congress ought to set aside some place where we can go and nobody can jump on us and beat us, neither lynch us nor Jim Crow us every day. Colored folks rate as much protection as a buffalo, or a deer" (181). Boyd, Simple's educated integrationist foil, first faults the plan for drawing a parallel between animals and humans: "Negroes are not wild," he asserts confidently. Yet in observing Simple's logical flaw, he misses Simple's important point. Precisely because blacks are human beings, they should be treated better than animals. Boyd admits, "You have a point there" (181), but immediately discerns another shortcoming in Simple's argument. When Simple says that one of the things he would like about living on a preserve is that he could "fight in peace and not get fined them high fines" (182), Boyd recoils: "You disgust me. I thought you were talking about a place where you could be quiet and compose your mind" (182). Again Boyd reacts against the racist stereotype that black men are physically aggressive.

In fact, however, the freedom to fight was suggested to Simple by a scene in the movie showing two elks locking horns. While Boyd would replace one behavioral cliché (black men fighting) with another (men meditating in nature), he fails to see that both prescriptions curtail freedom. Once again, Simple makes the more substantial point: "I would like a place where I could do both" (182). While Simple's ideas always sound regressive at first, he ultimately articulates a far more radical position than Boyd's; and he does so by rejecting the falsifying complexities Boyd raises. Boyd's willingness to view all racial issues as hopelessly intricate finally renders him ineffective and conservative. Simple's obstinacy, on the other hand, enables him to view all issues in black and white, so to speak. Indeed, "There Ought to Be a Law" introduces, in a back-handed way, a black separatist position that Simple holds throughout the stories. Far from capitulating to white racist stereotypes about African Americans, Simple advocates a complete break with the white world and, thus, a thorough rejection of white racist assumptions.[9]

When Simple tries his hand at poetry in two stories, we can begin to see how he embodies Hughes's conception of the poet. Ironically, in "Wooing the Muse" Simple is first inspired to compose poetry when he leaves the city to spend his vacation on the beach. Though the natural setting is a conventional pretext for poetry, Simple's verses ignore the romantic idealization of nature in favor of his characteristic realism regarding a subject that interests him more, human nature:

> Sitting under the trees
> With the birds and the bees
> Watching the girls go by. (*Best* 28)

In fact, he gently mocks Romantic clichés like "the birds and the bees" by incorporating such phrases into his irreverent lines. But it is precisely their status as clichés that Simple exploits, tossing off such lines as empty gestures toward figuration to contrast the way his poems barrel unmetaphorically toward their artless points (though his prose is highly figurative). And, of course, that second line is not just any cliché but a euphemism for sexual relations, and thus it receives a double reproof when Simple follows it with his blunt restatement, "Watching the girls go by."

---

[9] One might wonder how a character described as an "Everyman" or a "black separatist"—that is, as a stereotype—can break stereotypes. That is, how can black separatism resist stereotypes when it, *by definition*, carries racist stereotypes with it? This is a subtlety that would not interest Simple, who accepts the necessity of his own racism and rejects the idea that African Americans should "overcome" black nationalist stereotypes. As long as white racism prevails, he will resist in kind. See "Color on the Brain" (*Stakes* 106–110) for one of many exchanges between Simple and Boyd about this issue.

Predictably, Boyd misses the poem's own logic and faults the verse for its failure to realize conventional Anglo-American form: "You ought to have another rhyme. *By* ought to rhyme with *sky* or something" (28). Boyd cannot read the poem on its own terms but views it only as an unfinished quatrain composed (ideally) of two rhymed (aa/bb) couplets. Simple, on the other hand, sees no reason why form should exceed meaning: "I was not looking at no sky, as I told you in the poem. I was looking at the girls" (30).

Simple's second poem is a free-verse composition about racism; "This next one is a killer," he tells Boyd. "It's serious" (30). In it he compares the treatment of non-black immigrants in the United States with the mistreatment of African Americans:

I wonder how it can be
That Greeks, Germans, Jews,
Italians, Mexicans,
And everybody but me
Down South can ride in the trains,
Streetcars and busses
Without any fusses.
But when I come along—
Pure American—
They got a sign up
For me to ride behind:
    COLORED
My folks and my folks' folkses
And their folkses before
Have been here 300 years or more—
Yet any foreigner from Polish to Dutch
Rides anywhere he want to
And is not subject to such
Treatments as my fellow-men give me
In this Land of the Free. (30)

Again the poem is evaluated in terms of conventional literary standards when Joyce, Simple's fiancée, wants him "to change *folkses* to say *peoples*" in order to elevate its diction (31). But since Simple doesn't have an eraser, his original phrasing is preserved. This suggests another constituent feature of Simple's poetry: it is improvisational. Even when he writes poems, they are subject to the pressures of the immediate moment and cannot be polished or refined.

While the lack of an eraser might suggest the opposite, that the poem is fixed and unchangeable, it actually indicates that the process of composition—rather than the product (which is another matter and might receive revision at another time)—is spontaneous and improvisational. In fact, Simple thinks this poem should be longer, but he has to conclude it where he does because Joyce interrupts him during composition. And his sense that the poem should have been longer derives not from some external formal measure but from the integral relationship of structure and meaning. Boyd, on the other hand, thinks "It's long enough" because he doubts the poem's worth; but Simple asserts, "It's not as long as Jim Crow" (31).

After a lengthy discussion with Boyd about why he does not write more nature poems, Simple recites a third piece—a ten-stanza toast in the "counting rhymes" genre, structured in tercets (until the final stanza which is five lines) rhyming aab, like a blues stanza. The "b" line in each stanza is also a refrain line throughout, as in a ballad:

> When I get to be ninety-one
> And my running days is done,
> Then I will do better. (33)

Simple has concocted this toast as a retort to people who tell him, as Boyd has just done, "You should be old enough to know better." Simple distinguishes between "knowing" and "doing":

> "I might be old enough to know better, but I am not old enough to *do* better," said Simple. "Come on in the bar and I will say you a toast I made up the last time somebody told me just what you are saying now about doing better. . . . That's right bartender, two beers for two steers. . . . Thank you! . . . Pay for them, chum! . . . Now, here goes. Listen fluently." (33)

Several points in this passage bear upon Simple's poetic practice. Most important is the assertion that recognizing (knowing) social or literary conventions need not result in enacting them (doing). When Simple orders "two beers for two steers," he playfully supports this by infusing the poetical (by virtue of the rhymes) into the mundane as easily as he has infused the mundane into the poetical. Finally, when Simple cautions Boyd to "Listen fluently," he coins a phrase that will appear again and again in the stories, whenever Simple suspects that habitual ways of "reading" will obstruct the proper reception of his compositions. The odd phrase pulls artist and audience together, insisting that writer and reader accompany each other in a new literacy. "Listen fluently" also introduces orality, and appropriately so, since it precedes the toast, an oral composition, and thus widens the scope of poetry. As we have seen, many of Simple's poetic models are African-American folk forms—ballads, blues, toasts—genres that can claim written *and* oral status. Certainly Hughes, like Simple, "knows" about literary convention but chooses to "do" things his own way.

The opposition of correctness as knowledge and correctness as action (in the context of poetry, "action" means writing truthfully) is central to "Grammar and Goodness," another story that treats Simple's poetic production. Simple's formulation of this borders on the nonsensical, like many of his wise sayings: "It is better to *do* right than to write right" (*Stakes* 182). Simple reads two poems to the narrator (who in this story is apparently not Boyd). The first is one that Joyce and Boyd have edited. Its conclusion uneasily renders Boyd's accommodationist perspective in Simple's belligerent style:

> Now, listen, white folks:
> In line with Rev. King
> Down in Montgomery—
> Also because the Bible
> Says I must—
> In spite of bombs and buses,
> *I'm gonna love you.*
> I say, I'm gonna LOVE you—
> White folks, OR BUST! (181)

The "authorities"—Reverend King and the Bible (and behind them, certainly, Joyce and Boyd)—want Simple's poem to advocate loving the enemy.

However, this conciliatory theme is gainsaid by the imperative construction, the screaming capital letters, the allusions to white violence, and the threatening last line (which comes off as a warning to whites to *be* lovable rather than as a promise on Simple's part to love them "in spite" of themselves). Despite these obvious contradictions, the narrator extricates a coherent "message" from the piece by ignoring its style, and doubts whether Simple could have written such a poem: "You never wrote a poem that logical all by yourself in life" (181). Simple admits this freely and offers another, unedited, poem in its place; it is no surprise when it completely contradicts the first one. It begins,

> In the North
> The Jim Crow line
> Ain't clear—
> But it's here!

and ends,

> Up North Jim Crow
> Wears an angel's grin—
> But still he sin.
> I swear he do!
> Don't you? (181)

Though the narrator agrees with the sentiment of this poem, he chides Simple "for the grammar" (182). Simple once again rejects the notion that poems must meet formal standards, claiming, "If I get the sense right . . . the grammar can take care of itself" (182). Both "Wooing the Muse" and "Grammar and Goodness" repudiate the aesthetics of traditional poetry, especially adherence to conventional forms, elevation of diction, preference for written rather than oral forms, the necessity of polish and finish, and the subordination of content to form.

Simple is thus a folk poet in the African and African-American traditions. His poems are communal, colloquial, and often improvisational. When he uses existing verse forms, he chooses ballads, blues, toasts, and spirituals. Moreover, his speech is rendered lyrical through a high content of figuration and internal rhyme.[10] In addition to his status as folk poet, however, Simple is the embodiment of—and, considering his life span, perhaps the defender of—Langston Hughes's aesthetic program. His name, an epigrammatic poem in its own right, captures this aspect of the character.

In "Family History" Simple explains his highly suggestive name:

> "Grandpa's name was Jess, too. So I am Jesse B. Semple.
>
> "What does the *B* stand for?"
>
> "Nothing. I just put it there myself since they didn't give me no initial when I was born. I am really Jess Semple."
>
> (*Speaks* 179)

Simple's name invokes his family history, a heritage that the story reveals is multi-racial. His name, then, links him to a diverse cultural past and thereby at least superficially legitimates him as a representative figure. A second interesting feature of his name is the self-defining middle initial "B." He says the "B" stands for nothing, but knowing him, we wonder if it doesn't signify

---

[10] In "Cocktail Sip," for example, Boyd's quotations of Elizabethan poetry are juxtaposed with Simple's rhyming prose: "Zarita is strictly a after-hours gal—great when the hour is late, the wine is fine, and mellow whiskey has made you frisky" (*Wife* 47).

"black." Or, it may derive from another story, "Bop," in which he explains to Boyd that the difference between the prefixes "*Re* and *Be*" (in "Re-Bop" and "Be-Bop") is that the "Be" signifies "the real thing like the colored boys play" (*Wife* 56). In such a reading, the middle initial "B" might indicate the integrity of self-authorship, a prerequisite for being an authentic representative of his larger culture. Even more suggestive are the puns involved in Simple's names. By giving himself the middle initial he transforms his given name from a negative description of himself—Jess Semple ("just simple")—into an imperative statement—Jess B. Semple ("just be simple"). The revised name, then, issues a commanding motto for Hughes's poetic program. And finally, "Semple" may also be an ironic appropriation of the middle name of Aimee Semple McPherson, the evangelist, who became a vicious and outspoken opponent of Hughes during the early forties.[11] It would be sweet revenge to name his irreverent, black-nationalist bard after a white evangelist who tried to censor and, failing that, excoriated Hughes's poetry.

Simple's provocative name, his rich and original use of language, his obstinate literalism, his radical politics, and his eccentric appearance distinguish him as a poet figure and associate him with a long line of poetic simpletons—most important, with Shakespeare's fools. This is especially obvious in a story like "Cocktail Sip," where Boyd says Simple sounds like an Elizabethan poet, or "Midsummer Madness," in which Simple composes pithy proverbs. Like a Shakespearean fool, the Hughesian bard often encodes wisdom in nonsense.[12] Indeed, the cardinal point of the Simple stories is the wisdom of simplicity—a precept that, when applied to poetry, demands a daring aesthetic program.

Shakespeare in Harlem (1942), roughly contemporary with the Simple period, self-consciously engages in wooing Simple's muse. The volume is exemplary for two reasons: first, because it declares itself to be "A book of light verse," and second, because it has been largely overlooked by critics (the latter point undoubtedly due to the former). That is, its outspoken aesthetic recalcitrance has almost certainly doomed it to critical neglect. To read *Shakespeare in Harlem* we need an interpretative practice that accommodates these poems on their own terms, one that strives, as Simple would say, to "listen fluently."

---

[11]   Rampersad explains McPherson's antagonism to Hughes in chapter 14 of his second volume: "McPherson had a specific reason to harass Hughes. She was one of the allegedly fraudulent ministers of religion mentioned by name in his 'Goodbye Christ'" (390).

[12]   For discussions of the fool that emphasize the wisdom of his simplicity, see Welsford, Willeford, Weimann, and Goldsmith.

From the prefatory note at the front of the book,

> A book of light verse. Afro-Americana in the blues mood. Poems syncopated and variegated in the colors of Harlem, Beale Street, West Dallas, and Chicago's South Side.
>
> Blues, ballads, and reels to be read aloud, crooned, shouted, recited, and sung. Some with gestures, some not—as you like. None with a far-away voice (viii)

to "A Note on the Type" on the last page of the book,

> The headings are set in Vogue Extra-Bold, a typeface designed in our time with the aim to express the utmost simplicity (125)

Shakespeare in Harlem equates the poetic with the simple. It declares itself to contain merely "light verse," "Afro-*Americana*"—a collection of folk materials—rather than high art. Like much of Hughes's canon, this book will employ folk forms—"blues, ballads, and reels"—that common readers are already familiar with from the oral culture. Indeed, the poet encourages readers to make the poems their own: they should be "read aloud, crooned, shouted, recited, and sung." Further, they can be acted out, "Some with gestures, some not." The preface, then, casts readers in the role of performers who will interpret the poems "as [they] like." The allusion to *As You Like It* is the first oblique reference to the namesake of the book. Yet this Shakespeare, *in Harlem*, is near at hand, colloquial, folksy; he does not speak with the "far-away voice" of Elizabethan England or literary convention or classical poetry. Even his typeface expresses the "utmost simplicity."

But the appropriation of Shakespeare into simplicity in Harlem is not merely an adjustment undertaken for the audience, nor is it entirely a political maneuver. When Shakespeare goes to Harlem, he faces a crisis of language that is figured forth in extreme simplicity. The material and psychological conditions of Harlem as depicted here (elsewhere Hughes emphasizes its many positive aspects)—poverty, hunger, violence, lack of opportunity, unfathomable despair—render him almost speechless; it is only through the fool, conventionally a voice of simplicity amid overwhelming complexity, that the poet maintains expression. Like Virginia Woolf's imaginative "reconstruction" of the life of Julia Shakespeare in *A Room of One's Own*, in which she tries to imagine what would have been the fate of Shakespeare's sister (that is, of a talented female poet in the sixteenth century), Hughes is to some extent exploring what Shakespeare's fate would be were he an unemployed African American in twentieth-century Harlem.

Little wonder, then, that the title poem—in which we first hear how Shakespeare sounds in Harlem—is half nonsense:

Hey ninny neigh!
And a hey nonny noe!
Where, oh, where
Did my sweet mama go?

Hey ninny neigh
With a tra-la-la-la!
They say your sweet mama
Went home to her ma. (111)

The poem's nonsense syllables, as might be expected, echo a song from *As You Like It* which two pages sing in honor of the fool's engagement:

It was a lover and his lass,
  With a hey, and a ho, and a hey nonino,
That o'er the green cornfield did pass
  In springtime, the only pretty ringtime,
When birds do sing, hey ding a ding, ding.
Sweet lovers love the spring. (V.iii.15–20)

Shakespeare in Harlem reverses this song: love cannot be idealized through images of springtime and green fields. *As You Like It* itself ridicules romantic equations about love, nature, and the simple life, and the nonsense syllables in the pages' song suggest the fatuousness of those idealized formulations. In the Hughes poem, by contrast, the allusion to Shakespeare seems to marshal the linguistic resources of the fool. Here the nonsense, rather than echoing the mindless babble of the clichéd lyrics, disrupts the portentousness of the lines that communicate the loss of love. Indeed, the first two lines of nonsense in each quatrain seem almost to make possible the utterance of the final two lines that admit loss.

The structure of the stanzas, then, which move from nonsense to sense, suggests that the incantatory energy of the nonsense—deriving from rhymes, alliteration, exclamation marks, and most of all from the liberating effects of non-referential language—is necessary in order to accommodate the painful reality of the sense lines. The word "ninny" in Hughes's stanzas can thus be read simultaneously as a nonsense utterance and a direct address to the fool, "Hey, Ninny." In both cases the special capacities of foolishness are invoked. Similarly, the literal "no" that is released in the nonsensical "nonny noe" provides an aural negation of the otherwise ineluctable misfortune of the sense lines.

And though the poem sounds somewhat whimsical, lost love is not a comic subject in *Shakespeare in Harlem*. The "un-sonnet sequence" that opens the book (another revision of Shakespeare), "Seven Moments of Love," demonstrates what the rest of the book will reiterate: that to be abandoned by a lover is to be cast deeper into poverty. "Supper Time" moves from poverty as an image of loneliness to poverty as the literal result of being alone:

> I look in the kettle, the kettle is dry.
> Look in the bread box, nothing but a fly.
> Turn on the light and look real good!
> I would make a fire but there ain't no wood.
> Look at that water dripping in the sink.
> Listen at my heartbeats trying to think.
> Listen at my footprints walking on the floor.
> That place where your trunk was, ain't no trunk no more.
> Place where your clothes hung's empty and bare.
> Stay away if your want to, and see if I care!
> If I had a fire I'd make me some tea
> And set down and drink it, myself and me.
> Lawd! I got to find me a woman for the WPA—
> Cause if I don't they'll cut down my pay.

The un-sonnet sequence, indeed the entire book, treats love as a social rather than merely a private problem. Abandoned lovers are exposed to hunger and cold, to diminished wages and status. Details like the dry kettle, the empty breadbox, and the lack of firewood function simultaneously as metaphors for the speaker's isolation and as factual examples of the hardships he will face living on one income.

The title poem begins a process of recontextualization of private life that the rest of the book develops. In "Shakespeare in Harlem" a speaker registers his loss of love in the first quatrain and another person answers him with the reports of still other people ("they say") in the second quatrain. The poem, in a section of the book called "Lenox Avenue," obviously invokes the voices of the people living along the street. A man arrives home, discovers his partner is gone, asks where she went, and is answered by a crowd of neighbors that she went home to her mother. The communal nature of the event is further registered in the appellation "sweet mama" and in the lover's retreat to her own "ma." This is clearly a family affair, not the isolated nuclear family of suburbia but the extended family of a population that is shifting from the rural south to the urban north. (The Harlem resident's responsibility to aid even remote family members who move north is a repeated theme of the Simple stories.) Romance in this context is not the usual stuff of sonnets but a relationship modeled on the family, as the similarity between the terms "sweet mama" and "ma" indicates. The speaker's "sweet mama" has not left for independence or romance but has retreated to another community, where she will receive care: to her family. There can be little doubt that she is shrinking from the kind of hardships that the "Supper Time" speaker faces.

The poem's simplicity, then, has a great deal of work to do. The nonsense lines allude to a tradition of empty love sentiments even as they also tap the special verbal resources of the fool. The plurality of voices situates love as a public issue. The appellations "sweet mama" and "ma" suggest a paradigm of need and dependence that love can support but not conquer. Though the speaker may to some extent employ nonsense in an effort at "laughing to keep from crying," this cannot wholly account for the poem. After all, this is Shakespeare, a master of the oxymoron and paradox; that he resorts to nonsense and repetition indicates that his relocation to Harlem has taken a heavy linguistic toll.

"Shakespeare in Harlem" probably has echoes of another fool's song. King Lear's Fool advises that nonsense is an appropriate response (it is the sign, in fact, of some vestige of sense) to the extreme emotional and physical hardships that Lear and the Fool experience on the stormy heath:

> He that has and a little tiny wit,
> With a heigh-ho, the wind and the rain,
> Must make content with his fortunes fit,
> For the rain it raineth every day. (III.ii.74–77)

The logic of the Fool's song turns on the double use of "little tiny wit": it argues that he who has a shred of sense left will employ a bit of humor to accept his situation, no matter how horrible it seems. The association of the fool's perspective with wisdom is here and elsewhere abbreviated in the word "wit" that refers at once to humor, to knowledge, and, most important, to a quality that humor and knowledge combined may inspire: ingenuity. In *As You Like It* Rosalind tells Touchstone what is true for nearly all of Shakespeare's fools at one time or another, "Thou speak'st wiser than thou art ware of" (II.iv.55). Hughes's simpletons are blood brothers to Shakespeare's fools.

The wisdom and ingenuity of the Ninny become apparent when we contrast two of the poems in *Shakespeare in Harlem*. In "Kid Sleepy" the title character, like Melville's Bartleby the Scrivener, prefers not to participate in life. To all of the speaker's efforts at imaginatively resuscitating him, Kid Sleepy responds, "I don't care":

Listen, Kid Sleepy,
Don't you want to get up
And go to work down-
Town somewhere
At six dollars a week
For lunches and car fare?

Kid Sleepy said,
I don't care. (24)

The prospect of working for a pittance, of earning just enough money to continue going to work, does not inspire Kid Sleepy. The speaker of "*If*-ing," on the other hand, is brimming with optimism and energy, though he has no more material resources than Kid Sleepy does. He has, instead, verbal ones:

If I had some small change
I'd buy me a mule,
Get on that mule and
Ride like a fool.

If I had some greenbacks
I'd buy me a Packard,
Fill it up with gas and
Drive that baby backward.

If I had a million
I'd get me a plane
And everybody in America'd
Think I was insane.

But I ain't got a million,
Fact is, ain't got a dime—
So just by *if*-ing
I have a good time! (32)

The difference between Kid Sleepy and this speaker is that the second speaker, as he proudly admits in stanza one, is a fool. He can acknowledge that he "ain't got a dime," but that "fact" is countered by another, more important, fact: he has had a good time.

Kid Sleepy, as his name indicates, has utterly succumbed to hardship, while the "*If*-ing" speaker has turned nonsense into a survival strategy. And notably that strategy is a linguistic game that finds new uses for even the most apparently unavailing words. The very contingency of the word "if" renders it susceptible to transformation. The fool Touchstone in *As You Like It* recognizes a similar indeterminacy in the word. Touchstone explains that quarrels can be resolved not by determining the truth or falsity of conflicting claims but by rejecting these inflexible categories:

> All these [quarrels] you may avoid but the Lie Direct, and you may avoid that too, with an If. I knew when seven justices could not take up a quarrel, but when the parties were met themselves, one of them thought but of an If: as, "If you said so, then I said so"; and they shook hands and swore brothers. Your If is the only peacemaker. Much virtue in If. (V.iv.96–103)

Hughes's speaker also has discovered the virtue in "if," and he exploits its contingency in order to imagine a better life.[13] Further, the speaker's word game employs rhyme, alliteration, metaphor, and rhetorical extravagance in order to conjure linguistic wealth. Kid Sleepy's response to poverty and unproductive work is more sensible than the second speaker's, but it is killing him. His name tells us he is on the brink of unconsciousness, he drowses in the harmful sun throughout the poem, and, most troubling, he has almost no language. His final utterance, the one that ends the poem and probably finishes off Kid Sleepy himself, lacks a subject and verb—lacks, that is, subjectivity and thus the capacity to act: *"Rather just / stay here"* (25). The *"If-ing"* speaker, by contrast, uses "I" nine times in his short poem and not only employs a range of action verbs but creates the most crucial one himself. Indeed, "coining" the word *"if-ing"* is another way he amasses his imaginary fortune.

These two poems suggest that the simpleton's penchant for verbal play saves him because it makes linguistic production possible. When Shakespeare gets to Harlem, he is dumbstruck. Having recourse to the voice of the fool is how he continues to write poetry. What I have been calling his crisis of language is an important theme in these and other poems. It is also, however, a structural principle in the volume. The book consists of eight sections of poetry, four of which have generic designations that are anticipated in the preface: "Blues for Men," "Mammy Songs," "Ballads," and "Blues for Ladies." Two other titles emphasize locale rather than genre: "Death in

---

13 In his chapter on *Henry IV, Part I*, Holland makes a similar point, describing Falstaff's way of using "if" as a habit of speech that liberates him from the world of responsibilities and permits him to enter a "world of imaginings" (119).

Harlem" and "Lenox Avenue" (the street where Simple's hangout is located). All these sections answer to the interests of simplicity in their folk forms, common speakers, colloquial diction, everyday concerns, and uncomplicated ideas. Even more interesting are the first two sections: "Seven Moments of Love: An Un-Sonnet Sequence in Blues" and "Declarations" identify forms that are far simpler than ballads and blues: "moments," "declarations," a "statement," and one "little lyric." These new designations all emphasize brevity, bluntness, and simplicity, and they all take the thematics of simplicity to the structural level. As we will see, the poems themselves function like little elemental chunks of poetry that resist complication and elaboration. If we can find ways to read these atomic lyrics, we will have begun to achieve fluency in Hughes's poetry of simplicity.

I will conclude, then, by looking at several such poems in the "Declarations" section. The section title warns that these poems are not meditative or subtle in content, not figurative or lyrical in form. Instead, they are blurtings that make poetry out of the obvious or even the obtuse. "Hope," for example, reveals that the speaker's sense of possibility depends in an ironic way on her or his impoverished mental and linguistic resources:

Sometimes when I'm lonely,
Don't know why,
Keep thinkin' I won't be lonely
By and by. (16)

It is precisely the speaker's not knowing that makes hope possible. To know more, to think this out more thoroughly would surely mean the eradication of all hope. The speaker's language supports the sense that inarticulateness is bliss; the last line, "By and by," is a phrase from spirituals and hymns, songs that turn from misery toward hope by positing another time when suffering will be alleviated and even rewarded.

The speaker seems not to know where this formulation originates, but it is nevertheless part of her or his severely limited verbal repertoire. The exhaustion and vagueness of "by and by," ironically, make it efficacious. Two insubstantial words create hope by putting the concreteness of a harsh reality (now) into relation with the abstractness of a better future time (then); and in the process the phrase conjures up an in-between realm of relation even though it cannot visualize hope in more decisive terms. Further, "by" is a homonym for the "bye" in "goodbye" and lends a sense of finality that shuts down further thought and thus staves off despair. "Hope" is achieved, then, by dwelling in an intellectual and linguistic limbo, by waiting in some state that is neither "here" nor "there"—a provisional state characterized by verbal simplicity. "By and by" defers all the mental and linguistic processes that would inevitably lead to the negation of hope.

"Statement" announces its simplicity in its title. And, true to its name, it offers only this bare fact:

> Down on '33rd Street
> They cut you
> Every way they is. (28)

The speaker making this statement has no time for pondering the by-and-by, subject as he is to the perils of the present moment. The knife-wielding, anonymous "they" are not just the perpetrators of street violence but also other evils—hunger, poverty, unemployment, disappointment—that produce physical violence (as the dialect "they" for "there" suggests). The ubiquitousness of "they" and "every way" demands the full attention of this speaker, who can only state or declare the bald truth about life on 133rd Street. The conditions of his existence prevent him from analyzing, lyricizing, or elaborating his plight. The reader, of course, can do these things; in fact, to listen fluently *is* to analyze these brief utterances and elaborate recognitions and insights that move beyond them. But "Statement" itself remains a hard fact and thus an obstinate form that articulates the exigencies of Harlem.

Finally, "Little Lyric" self-consciously demonstrates the way that poetry will be altered when Shakespeare gets to Harlem: The poem's epigraph insists parenthetically that this little lyric is "*Of Great Importance*":

> I wish the rent
> Was heaven sent. (21)

What is lost in reproducing the poem here is the way the tiny couplet is engulfed by the rest of the page. The white space that ominously surrounds it is as crucial to a reading of the poem as its two lines are. "Little Lyric" says visually that the sigh of desire expressed in the poem has been nearly extinguished by the vast emptiness around it. The visual hopelessness and fragility of the poem on the page are translated into language in the poem proper. Like "by and by," the idiomatic phrase "heaven sent" does not express a real confidence in divinity to pay the rent miraculously but rather employs the unavailing concept of heaven to figure forth dumb luck. Since there is obviously no heaven (as the hardships and injustices of Harlem seem to indicate), or at least no heaven that is willing to intervene, wishing "the rent / Was heaven sent" is merely an ironic way to acknowledge that the rent will not be paid. Again the brevity of the poem, the sufficiency of its perfect rhymes, and the elemental simplicity of its point are features that defy further elaboration within the poem.

The "Little Lyric" enacts the near loss of language. It reveals in an extreme form what all the other poems in the volume suggest—that utter simplicity is the only adequate response to a dislocated life in an urban ghetto in a racist country. Simplicity, as we have seen, sometimes takes the form of nonsense and foolishness and sometimes takes the form of brevity and obviousness. Both manifestations of Hughes's aesthetics of simplicity forgo the complexities of "great poetry" in order to express something that is "of great importance." Such poems would rather do right than write right.

WORKS CITED

Baldwin, James. "Sermon and Blues." Mullen 85–87.

Goldsmith, R. H. *Wise Fools in Shakespeare.* East Lansing: Michigan State UP, 1955.

Hollands, Norman N. *The Shakespearean Imagination: A Critical Introduction.* Bloomington: Indiana UP, 1964.

Hudson, Theodore R. "Technical Aspects of the Poetry of Langston Hughes." *Black World* (1973): 24–45.

Hughes, Langston. *The Best of Simple.* New York: Hill, 1961.

———. *The Big Sea: An Autobiography.* New York: Knopf, 1940.

———. *Five Plays by Langston Hughes.* Bloomington: Indiana UP, 1968.

———. "The Happy Journey of 'Simply Heavenly.'" *New York Herald-Tribune* 18 Aug. 1957, sec. 4: 1+.

———. *The Langston Hughes Reader.* New York: Braziller, 1958.

———. "The Negro Artist and the Racial Mountain." *The Nation* CXXII (1926): 692–94.

———. "The Negro Speaks of Rivers." *The Norton Anthology of American Literature.* Ed. Nina Baym et al. 2nd ed. New York: Norton, 1985.

———. *Selected Poems of Langston Hughes.* New York: Vintage, 1974.

———. *Shakespeare in Harlem.* New York: Knopf, 1942.

———. "Simple and Me." *Phylon* 6 (1945): 349–52.

———. *Simple Speaks His Mind.* New York: Simon, 1950.

———. *Simple Stakes a Claim.* New York: Rinehart, 1953.

———. *Simple's Uncle Sam.* New York: Hill, 1965.

———. *Simple Takes a Wife.* New York: Simon, 1953.

———. *Simply Heavenly. Five Plays by Langston Hughes.* Bloomington: Indiana UP, 1968.

———. "Who Is Simple?" *The Best of Simple.* New York: Hill, 1961. vii–viii.

Jemie, Onwuchekwa. *Langston Hughes: An Introduction to the Poetry.* New York: Columbia UP, 1976.

Miller, R. Baxter. *The Art and Imagination of Langston Hughes.* Lexington: UP of Kentucky, 1989.

Mullen, Edward J. *Critical Essays on Langston Hughes.* Boston: Hall, 1986.

Rampersad, Arnold. *The Life of Langston Hughes, Volume II: 1941–1967.* New York: Oxford UP, 1988.

Redding, Saunders. "Old Form, Old Rhythms, New Words." Mullen 73–74.

Welsford, Enid. *The Fool: His Social and Literary History.* London: Faber, 1935.

Wiemann, Robert. *Shakespeare and the Popular Tradition in the Theater: Studies in the Social Dimension of Dramatic Form and Function.* Baltimore: Johns Hopkins UP, 1978.

Willeford, William. *The Fool and His Scepter: A Study in Clowns, Jesters, and Their Audiences.* Evanston: Northwestern UP, 1969.

HERMAN BEAVERS

Dead Rocks and Sleeping Men: Aurality
in the Aesthetic of Langston Hughes
(1992)

In his 1940 autobiography, *The Big Sea,* Langston Hughes discusses the circumstances that lead him, at the puerile age of 19, to the creation of his
poem, "The Negro Speaks of Rivers." The poem came into being during
a trip to Mexico, Hughes writes, "when [he] was feeling very bad."[1] Thus,
he connects poetic inspiration and emotional turbulence, both of which
stemmed from his attempt to understand his father's self-hatred. He relates,
"All day on the train I had been thinking about my father and his strange
dislike of his own people. I didn't understand it because I was a Negro, and
I liked Negroes very much" (54). What is striking about the end of this passage is that one finds Hughes adopting a posture both inside and outside the
race: he does not make a statement of self-love (e.g. I like myself), rather he
indicates through a kind of reflexivity, that he has self-worth. In short, he is
unable to articulate self-valuation, he can only construct his positionality as
the mirror opposite of his father's racial feeling. But then Hughes shifts the
subject and recalls that "one of the happiest jobs [he] ever had," was the time
he spent working behind the soda fountain of a refreshment parlor, in "the
heart of the colored neighborhood" in Cleveland. He offers this description:

> People just up from the South used to come in for ice cream and sodas and
> watermelon. And I never tired of *hearing* their talk, *listening* to thunderclaps
> of their laughter, to their troubles, to their discussions of the war and the men
> who had gone to Europe from the Jim Crow South, their complaints over the
> high rent and the long overtime hours that brought what seemed big checks,
> until the weekly bills were paid. (54, my emphasis)

I quote this passage at length to point to the disjointed quality Hughes's narrative assumes. In one chapter, we find the self-hatred of his father, his own
admiration for the recuperative powers of newly arrived Southern blacks,
and the act of composing a famous poem. The elements that form Hughes's

---

[1] Langston Hughes, *The Big Sea* (1940; New York: Hill and Wang, 1963) 54. All subsequent
    references to this text are from this volume.

account can be read, at least on a cursory level, as an attempt to demonstrate that his "best poems were written when [he] felt the worst" (54). This notwithstanding, what I would like to propose is that we can place the poem into an aesthetic frame that brings these three disparate elements into a more geometrical alignment.

Hughes's autobiographical account can be found in the middle of a chapter entitled, "I've Known Rivers." Having established his father as someone he neither understands nor wishes to emulate, the autobiography paints the older man as an outsider, not only geographically, but spiritually as well. That Hughes would discuss his father in relation to such an important poem, alludes to body travel of a different sort than that which he undertakes in this chapter of his autobiography. Moving further away from Cleveland, the geographical space where he encountered the individuals he describes as "the gayest and bravest people possible . . ." (54), Hughes elides the distance his father has put between himself and other blacks. He resists the impulses that lead to the latter's self-imposed exile: he is immersed in a vernacular moment and simultaneously peripheral to that moment. What differentiates the younger Hughes is that he listens to the voices of the folk and is "empowered rather than debilitated" by what he hears.[2]

In composing the poem, Hughes looks at "the great muddy river flowing down toward the heart of the South" (*The Big Sea* 55). While he suggests that it is his gaze—looking out of the train window at the Mississippi—that initiates composition, I would assert that what catalyzes his act of writing is the act of recovering the spoken word. A point emphasized, moreover, by the fact that he recounts a moment where he is listener rather than speaker.

Later in the autobiography, Hughes relates, in much less detail, the events which lead to his poem, "The Weary Blues." There, he states, simply: "That winter, I wrote a poem called "The Weary Blues," about a piano-player I heard in Harlem . . ." (92). Again, Hughes's poetic composition moves forward from an aural moment where, as with "The Negro Speaks of Rivers," he is an outsider. Arnold Rampersad alludes to this when he observes:

> . . . [I]n his willingness to stand back and record, with minimal intervention
> as a craftsman, aspects of the drama of black religion or black music, Hughes

---

[2] Arnold Rampersad, *The Life of Langston Hughes, Volume I: 1902–1941: I, Too, Sing America*, 2 vols. (New York: Oxford UP, 1986) 1: 64.

had clearly shown already that he saw his *own art as inferior* [my emphasis] to that of either black musicians or religionists. . . . At the heart of his sense of inferiority . . . was the knowledge that he stood to a great extent *outside* the culture he worshipped.[3]

Rampersad concludes that Hughes's sense of alienation resulted from the fact that "his life had been spent away from consistent, normal involvement with the black masses whose affection and regard he craved" (64–5).

This trajectory repeats itself in "The Weary Blues." Rampersad intimates as much in his description of the poem's inception: "And then one night in March [of 1922], in a little cabaret in Harlem, he finally *wrote himself and his awkward position accurately into a poem* [my emphasis]" (65). This assessment calls our attention to an important consideration, namely, that Hughes's aural aesthetic employs the externality he felt in the African American community. That he was a writer and not a musician, preacher, or dancer meant that his artistic project was to record artistic expression, to amplify the African American vernacular speech event for the rest of the world to hear. Further, Hughes's sense that his literary representation of the folk was inferior, mere imitation, in turn means that he was positioned, as artist, at a distance from the "real source," almost as if he were a loudspeaker serving as a medium through which sound travels, rather than the source itself. In becoming comfortable with this role, Hughes traversed repeatedly the conceptual distance necessary to create authentic representations of black speech. Hence, as he achieved a greater place among the African American intellectual elite, the distance increased between him and the masses he sought to portray. Nonetheless, as his aesthetic sensibility crystallized, his conceptual movement was *toward* them.

This is evidenced by the fact that Hughes's Simple character resulted from a conversation he shared with a factory worker and his girlfriend in a Harlem bar in 1943. Intrigued as he listened to the exchange, Hughes used the qualities he discerned from the conversation to create the character, who first appeared in his column for *The Chicago Defender.*[4] Constructed as a dialogue between a narrator speaking in standard English and Jesse B. Semple (or Simple), who spoke in a more colorful, Southern idiom, the columns

---

[3] Rampersad 64–65. My emphasis.

[4] Rampersad, *The Life of Langston Hughes, Volume II: 1941–1967: I Dream a World,* 2 vols. (New York: Oxford UP, 1988) 2: 61–62.

work out Hughes's passionate desire to honor the self-redemptive power found in the African American community. Thus, Simple became a vehicle for giving voice to the nature of his artistic project; indeed, it is he who articulates the necessity, as if it were a constant reminder to Hughes, to listen "eloquently."

If the ability to "listen eloquently" characterizes Hughes's attempts to celebrate "the folk," one also finds him creating stories that illustrate the ways that African American culture is objectified because people, particularly whites, fail to understand what African American voices articulate. In Hughes's collection of stories, *The Ways of White Folks*, for example, we find stories like "Slaves on the Block," where the Carraways are described as "people who went in for Negroes." When their maid's nephew, Luther, arrives at their home, they are immediately attracted to him as the ultimate exotic. Michael Carraway, as one who thinks "in terms of music," exclaims, "He's 'I Couldn't Hear Nobody Pray.'" Not only does Hughes suggest that Carraway confuses physicality and spirituality, but the song title signals his lack of aural dexterity as well.

In "The Blues I'm Playing," Mrs. Ellsworth takes on the role of benefactress for Oceola, a young black woman who is a gifted pianist. However, the investment leads her to believe that she can dictate what her protégé will play. Indeed, she can only "hear" Oceola when she plays classical music, despite the fact that she also plays the blues and spirituals. Tension develops between the two when the older woman, "really [begins] to hate jazz, especially on a grand piano." In short, Oceola is mute unless she capitulates to Mrs. Ellsworth's belief that classical music is "superior" to vernacular musical expression.

What both these stories suggest, through their dramatization of white aural incompetence, is that African American culture is self-constituted, discursive, and regenerative. In each, Hughes is positioned at the nexus of the two cultures to mediate the events, to encode what one reads in the stories as aural incompetence. At the end of "The Blues I'm Playing," Mrs. Ellsworth claims that marriage will "take all the music" out of Oceola. The latter responds by playing the blues, which symbolizes her rejection of what Hughes suggests is the bourgeoisie's inclination to compartmentalize experience in order to create art.

Herein lies an important consideration: that Hughes's aesthetic works out a trope that brings internality and externality into a state of opposition. One sees an example of how this unfolds in "The Weary Blues." The speaker in the poem documents the experience of listening to a piano player in Harlem play the blues. Steven Tracy's compelling argument asserts that the piano player and speaker are united by the performance.[5] I would like to argue to the contrary however. In my view, the poem works out Hughes's apprehension, his feeling that his ability to understand the emotions that generated this form of artistic expression was not on a par with the expression itself. This is indicated by the last line of the poem, where the speaker notes that the piano player "slept like a rock or a man that's dead." The key word here is "or," for it denotes the imprecision of the speaker's understanding. What the blues articulates is the simultaneous presence of the "tragic and comic aspects of the human condition."[6] Thus, the blues in the poem is not the conventional "either/or" condition configured within the Cartesian construct. Rather, the piano player, by metaphorizing loneliness has already chosen self-recovery.[7] The poem's last line, then, ignores the blues performer's ability to articulate pain and likewise to subsume it. That the speaker and the piano player never meet, or as Tracy asserts, "strike up a conversation, share a drink, or anything else," suggests that the experience does not rupture the speaker's externality. He never enters that space whereby the piano player is speaking for him, giving utterance to his loneliness. Finally, at no point in time does the speaker in the poem insert himself into the lyrics.[8]

---

[5] Steven Tracy, *Langston Hughes and the Blues.* (Urbana: U of Illinois P, 1988) 222–23.

[6] Ralph Ellison, "Blues People," *Shadow and Act* (New York: Vintage, 1972) 256. Consider also Ellison's definition of the blues, found in his essay, "Richard Wright's Blues," where he notes: "The blues is an impulse to keep the painful details and episodes of a brutal experience alive in one's aching consciousness, to finger its jagged grain, and to transcend it, not by the consolation of philosophy but by squeezing from it a near-tragic, near-comic lyricism. As a form, the blues is an autobiographical chronicle of personal catastrophe expressed lyrically." Ellison's definition allows me to invalidate Hughes's "or" at the end of "The Weary Blues," and to move towards the notion that he intentionally "misreads" the silence that comes in the poem when the piano player has "stopped playing and [gone] to bed." That he conjectures about the dualistic nature of the blues suggests that he is still outside, he does not move into the "zone of the sacred" that the blues represents.

[7] In her seminal essay, "The Blues Roots of Poetry," Sherley Anne Williams argues: "The internal strategy of the blues is action rather than contemplation; for the song itself is the creation of reflection." Michael S. Harper and Robert B. Stepto, eds. *Chant of Saints* (Urbana: U of Illinois P, 1979) 125.

[8] This would represent what Michael S. Harper refers to in his liner notes to the album, "John Coltrane" as "the communal nature of the relationship between blues singer and audience . . . which assumes 'we' even though the blues singer sings 'I.'" Williams 124.

What this implies is that "The Weary Blues" can also be read as an anti-Jazz Age poem. That is, a case can be made in which we need not equate the speaker in the poem with Hughes at all. While Hughes obviously had a strong desire to "link the lowly blues to formal poetry," locking him into the poem ignores its efficacy as cultural commentary. Given the increasing number of whites travelling to Harlem to be entertained in clubs like The Cotton Club, the poem can be seen as an attempt on Hughes's part to warn the community that African American expression was being appropriated by mainstream culture.[9]

The poem's structure enables this reading, if only because the speaker "quotes" the lyrics, but never allows his own voice to give way to them. Moreover, the speaker is "Down on Lenox Avenue . . ." which also, interestingly enough, marks the location of the Cotton Club and thus implies travel from downtown Manhattan. The I/he dichotomy Hughes establishes never collapses, which means that we can read the exteriority of the speaker as that which pertains to someone being entertained, who will leave Harlem after the performance is over. In this respect, the "or" in the last line calls our attention to the slippage that occurs when an understanding of the blues is lacking. That the speaker utters the possibility that the piano player has killed himself illustrates his failure to realize that the blues is performed reflection and not a preface to suicidal behavior.

If we return to the moment in his autobiography where Hughes is headed to Mexico towards his father, what is clear is that he circumvents his father's hatred of blacks by reconstituting the aural joy he feels in their midst. In short, Hughes's aesthetic rests on his need to assure his readership that if his writing spoke, both to and for them, it was because he took great pains to hear them. In his multivarious roles as poet, fiction writer, autobiographer, and columnist, Langston Hughes relates to the African American community as a speaker to be sure, but here the term is dualistic: the term alludes to the act of writing as both composition and amplification. As the Rampersad biography makes very clear, Hughes never elevated books over spoken forms of eloquence and his passion for writing flowed naturally from

---

[9] Hughes asserts this point when he observes: "White people began to come to Harlem in droves. For several years they packed the expensive Cotton Club on Lenox Avenue. But I was never there, because the Cotton Club was a Jim Crow club for gangsters and monied whites." If we refer back to the poem, then, it is clear that Hughes's speaker could easily have been one of that hoard. One might also consider that this poem anticipates a later Hughes poem in which he laments: "you've taken my blues and gone—/You sing 'em on Broadway/and you sing 'em in the Hollywood Bowl. . . ." *The Big Sea* 224–225.

the fact that he seized every opportunity to posit himself as a listener. *The Big Sea* begins, after all, with Hughes standing on the deck of the *S.S. Malone* (his pseudonym for the freighter, *West Hesseltine*) and throwing books into the sea (3).[10] "[B]ooks had been happening to me," he writes, "I was glad they were gone" (4). What this suggests is that Hughes never wanted to subordinate experience to literacy; books could not replace the value of improvisation. Although their disappearance from his life was temporary, one can imagine that that movement, like so many others in Hughes's life, led him towards what he so dearly loved to do: put his ear to the wind and serve as a witness for all there was to hear.

George B. Hutchinson

Langston Hughes and the "Other" Whitman
(1992)

By the "other" Whitman in my title I have in mind two distinct but related concepts. One comes from the title of an article published by Leandro Wolfson in 1978, "The Other Whitman in Spanish America," in which Wolfson criticizes the continued adoration of Whitman in Latin America, pointing out the inaccuracies in the Hispanic view of the North American poet. This "other" Whitman has been debunked and/or repressed (depending upon how you look at it) in the United States since the 1950s as part of the effort to bring his poetry into the academy during an era of formalism, hostility to political writing or propaganda, and emphasis upon confessional aspects of poetry. It was felt that Whitman had to be saved from his disciples as well as from the criticism of scholars who found his work to lack "form."

The second concept I have in mind is closer to Borges's, that of Whitman as a poetic "other" to all of us for the very reason that he is each one of us when we respond to his call, a ubiquitous signifier always slipping in and out of our embrace, an ecstatic moving always outside our attempts to fix a position for him. This "other" Whitman will always elude us because his

---

[10] In throwing books from Columbia into the sea, Hughes was likewise acting out the final break from his father, who had paid for him to attend. That the elder Hughes wanted Langston to "[acquire] a good business head," (*The Big Sea* 45) only drove him further towards being an artist.

otherness is fundamental to his own textual production. It is this more radical and mercurial otherness that has made him the most diversely appropriated American poet. For some reason, in Whitman's mirror many "others" to white, patriarchal American culture have seen themselves; the process of translating his voice has helped them to find their own. Langston Hughes certainly attested to this effect in his own career.

The association of Hughes with Whitman, I suspect, is less than obvious to most readers. If Whitman is often singled out as the archetypal (white male) American poet, Hughes's experiments with black-based idioms and aesthetic principles rooted in blues, ballads, and spirituals have had an incalculable effect upon the development of a distinctive African-American poetics. Yet, like Sterling Brown after him, even in writing his "folk" poems Hughes considered himself to be following out the implications of Whitman's poetic theory (Rampersad, 1:146). At various points in his long career, Hughes put together no fewer than three separate anthologies of Whitman's poetry (one of them for children), included several Whitman poems in an anthology on *The Poetry of the Negro,* wrote a poem entitled "Old Walt" for the one hundredth anniversary of *Leaves of Grass,* and repeatedly—in lectures, newspaper columns, and introductions—encouraged black Americans to read his work. He called Whitman "America's greatest poet" and spoke of *Leaves of Grass* as the greatest expression of "the real meaning of democracy ever made on our shores." Feeling that Whitman had been ignored and, in current parlance, marginalized by the custodians of culture, Hughes indeed attempted in his own way to canonize the poet he considered "the Lincoln of our Letters" (*Chicago Defender,* July 4, 1953).

The poems Hughes most liked are not the ones most taught today. For example, "Ethiopia Saluting the Colors," which has been called racist in content and hackneyed in form, Hughes praised as "the most beautiful poem in our language concerning a Negro subject," and he included it in *Poetry of the Negro.* His collaborator Harry T. Burleigh (an important black composer) even set the poem to music. "Song of the Open Road" and "Song of the Answerer" were two of his other favorites. Hughes admired the public poems that dramatized the singer's egalitarian ubiquity, his ability to permeate social boundaries, and his role as multiversal "answerer," which accounted, in Hughes's view, for Whitman's ability to portray black people realistically.

In "Song of the Answerer"—a poem that has rarely attracted the notice of scholars—the answerer knows that "Every existence has its idiom, every thing has an idiom and tongue . . . / He says indifferently and alike *How are you friend?* to the President at his levee, / And he says *Good-day my brother,* to Cudge that hoes in the sugar-field,/And both understand him and know that his speech is right" (31, 34–36). The egalitarian message and the specific reference to the black field-worker would have attracted Hughes at once. But two other characteristics also stand out. First is the importance of respecting the "idiom" of each existence. The answerer is able to resolve this idiom into his own tongue, which he then bestows upon people, who then translate that tongue back into their own even as they translate the answerer himself. "The English believe he comes of their English stock,/A Jew to the Jew he seems, a Russ to the Russ, usual and near, removed from none" (45–46). Whitman also allows for the possibility of multiple translations and thereby answers the objections of those, such as Doris Sommer, who claim that he tries to make us all equal by making us all mirror images of himself. On the contrary he demands that each of us make him a mirror image of *our* selves. As Hughes saw it, "his poems contain us all. The reader cannot help but see his own better self therein" (Perlman et al., 98). Whitman's specular answerer acts as a mediator between plural identities, reconciling pluralism with union—"One part does not counteract another part, he is the joiner, he sees how they join" (33). Hughes insisted that, in his masked performances, Whitman was able to project a voice, ventriloquistically, outside his own socially constructed role within American culture, a voice that resonated in the sensibilities of a tremendous range of writers throughout the world (*Chicago Defender,* Aug. 1, 1953).

Though precipitated by the specific ideological and social conflicts in which Whitman was immersed in the years leading up to the Civil War, the evident drive in the poems toward a resolution of those conflicts opens up a liminal, antistructural arena in which the very self is dismembered as it escapes all formulae. This semiotic shattering of the unity of the self in the process of textual production is matched by the exceedingly multivalent quality of Whitman's poetic language, the quality which helps account for its "translations" into so many different social contexts. On top of even these factors is the function of the unnamed second person within the very type of poems Hughes most admired—those like "Song of the Answerer" and "Song of the Open Road."

One reason Whitman's poetry has resonated in the sensibilities of black American writers is that in certain of his poems he uses the condition of the slave as representative of the condition of his audience. The "you" of his songs, if it is to apply to *all* readers, must apply to slaves, those most graphically denied the right to self-determination. The poem "To You (Whoever You Are)" at times seems directly addressed to a slave:

> None has done justice to you, you have not done justice
>   to yourself,
> None but has found you imperfect, I only find no
>   imperfection in you,
> None but would subordinate you, I only am he who will
>   never consent to subordinate you,
> I only am he who places over you no master, owner,
>   better, God, beyond what waits intrinsically in
>   yourself. (14–17)

Arguably, Whitman here distills the specific oppression of black people in the antebellum United States into a metaphor for the hidden condition of all people—"you, whoever you are." But his slave is not just any slave—his slave is the *most* enslaved, the one rejected by all others and even by himself or herself. Eschewing pity for admiration and love, the poet projects upon his reader, as by a shamanistic charm, a spiritual freedom that will ensure self-fulfillment: "The hopples fall from your ankles, you find an unfailing sufficiency,/Old or young, male or female, rude, low, rejected by the rest, whatever you are promulges itself" (44–45). A poem such as this virtually begs for appropriation to an African American frame of reference.

Hence, Hughes was not simply in *the* Whitman tradition (although he may have been happy with such a characterization); rather, he practiced an African-American–based poetic syncretism that Whitman's answerer explicitly invited: "The words of the true poems give you more than poems,/ They give you to form for yourself poems, religions, politics, war, peace, behavior, histories, essays, daily life, and every thing else,/ They balance ranks, colors, races, creeds, and the sexes" (75–77). The very nature of Hughes's absorption of Whitman was inevitably shaped by his "racial" identity and historical placement. In fact, it appears that by moving him toward an appreciation of the poetry of the common people, insisting on self-trust, and teaching "straying" from the teacher-poet himself, Hughes's demonic Whitman encouraged black cultural self-identification.

The very years in which Hughes grew close to the urban black community (having grown up largely removed from it) while determining to make his living as a poet were those in which he was most intensely under the spell of Whitman, as Arnold Rampersad's biography shows. Moreover, at a critical point in his life, when leaving the United States for Europe and Africa on a merchant ship, he threw overboard every book he owned except *Leaves of Grass*. "I had no intention of throwing that one away," he wrote in a passage from his autobiography (Rampersad, 1:72). By the time he returned to

America, Hughes had determined what his vocation would be. His absorption of Whitman was as thorough as that of any other North American poet of his generation. Even in describing the blues to Carl Van Vechten to help him with a preface to *The Weary Blues,* Hughes would slip effortlessly into a cadence, a mixture of idioms, and even the exact phrasing of "old Walt," stealing Whitman's evocation of sexual desire: "In the Gulf Coast Blues one can feel the cold northern snows, the memory of the melancholy mists of the Louisianna [*sic*] low-lands, the shack that is home, the worthless lovers with hands full of gimme, mouths full of much oblige, the eternal unsatisfied longings."

Hughes was the first African-American poet to sense the affinity between the inclusive "I" of Whitman (which Whitman claimed as his most important innovation—"the quite changed attitude of the ego, the one chanting or talking, towards himself and towards his fellow humanity" ("A Backward Glance," 564) and the "I" of the blues and even of the spirituals. The result of Hughes's appropriation of this triply descended "I" is amply demonstrated in one of his first published poems, "The Negro Speaks of Rivers":

> I've known rivers ancient as the world and old as the
>   flow of human blood in human veins.
>
> My soul has grown deep like the rivers.
>
> I bathed in the Euphrates when dawns were young.
> I built my hut near the Congo and it lulled me to sleep.
> I looked upon the Nile and raised the pyramids above it.
> I heard the singing of the Mississippi when Abe Lincoln
>   went down to New Orleans, and I've seen its muddy
>   bosom turn all golden in the sunset. (*Weary Blues,* 51)

Though Hughes would later, for the most part, turn away from the Whitmanesque style of free verse, the example of Whitman's break with traditional definitions of the poetic, his attempts to achieve an orally based poetics with the cadence and diction of the voice on the street, at the pond-side, or at the pulpit, provided a partial model for the young black poet looking for a way to sing his own song, which would be at the same time a song of his people.

Furthermore, Whitman's conception of the relationship between poet and community was fundamentally that in which Hughes came to believe: "In vain," Whitman had written, "will America seek successfully to tune any superb national song unless the heartstrings of the people start it from their own breasts—to be return'd and echoed there again." Hughes would not have to wait for the people to start the song from their breasts; it was ready-formed in the spirituals and blues, which he could justly regard as the most American of song genres available to modern poets. Moreover, these forms embodied the very sort of call-and-response pattern for which Whitman seemed to be asking. It would take Hughes's example (and later that of Zora Neale Hurston and Sterling Brown) to transform the dialect tradition into an uncompromising revelation of the folk-based African-American expressive arts, with a range, a flexibility, and a precision that had not yet found their way into poetry.

The "Epilogue" (later entitled "I, Too") of Hughes's first book, *The Weary Blues,* can be read in part as a signifying riff on "old Walt's" songs, forthrightly challenging American rituals of incorporation and exclusion while more subtly playing off of Whitman's "I Hear America Singing" with a dark minor chord.

> I, too, sing America
> I am the darker brother.
> They send me to eat in the kitchen
> When company comes . . . (109)

In the American family home, the "darker brother," disowned by white siblings, has been cast out of the common room to servants' space, where he nonetheless grows strong. The poem prophesies the transforming force of the black singer's particular challenge—on the basis of his own aesthetic standards—for the humanization of the white American audience: "They'll see how beautiful I am /And be ashamed,—/ I, too, am America." In this epilogue to his first collection—a poem with which he often concluded his poetry readings—Hughes registers his own distinctive poetic identity as both black and American. Simultaneously, he protests a *community*—even *family*—relationship with those across the color line and makes his claim as an heir to Whitman.

His second volume, *Fine Clothes to the Jew,* would show an even more radical break than *The Weary Blues* with past "literary" models by relying more exclusively upon the blues matrix for its aesthetic. Ironically, while the book was being blasted in the black press on genteel grounds and such intellectuals as Benjamin Brawley speculated that Hughes was pandering to the prurient interests of white folks, Hughes was invited to speak to the Walt Whitman Foundation about his poetry. Here, according to his biographer, he described "modern free verse, and his own work, as descending from Whitman's great example" (Rampersad, 1:146), an admission T. S. Eliot and Amy Lowell declined to make. At the same time, he emphasized his reliance upon the black folk tradition, which he characterized as the source of some of America's most distinctive aesthetic achievements. His very descent from Whitman demands difference from him, but difference within an American field. Hughes's liminal status—between white and black intellectual communities—freed him to explore new African-American literary forms.

Hughes had come to Whitman by way of such midwestern rebels as Carl Sandburg prior to the twenties. His was in most respects the democratic "transnationalist" and socialist Whitman pushed by Horace Traubel and other early disciples in the United States, followed by such influential figures as the French unanimist Léon Bazalgette, whose hagiographical study, *Walt Whitman,* had an enormous impact throughout Europe and Latin America, finally reacting back upon left-wing "cultural nationalists" in the United States. *Whitmanisme,* as the French called it, was a pervasive intercultural phenomenon (Betsy Erkkila) that embraced anti-imperialists in Europe (Romain Rolland) and the United States (*The Seven Arts* circle), as well as India (Rabindranath Tagore) and Latin America (José Martí, Rubén Dario) (see Grünzweig). The Hispanic reception of Whitman deserves particular attention here, for Hughes's connections with writers in the Caribbean and Latin America (and in Spain during its Civil War) were important in his career.

Whitman's influence upon such influential poets and revolutionaries as José Martí and Pablo Neruda is generally well known. Even as these socially engaged writers fought imperialism, they looked toward Whitman as a great New World forebear, the champion of democracy, social justice, and national self-determination. Fernando Alegría's account of the image of Whitman he'd had as a student at the University of Chile before World War II is broadly representative: "Whitman was the defender of liberty and the spirit, the enemy of prejudice, the proud sustainer of the purity and excellence of the artistic work, the chanter of youth, of life in contact with nature, the older brother of the workers, the romantic apostle of the persecuted and exploited" (9–10). Such views of Whitman have remained very strong to this day and have even come back to influence North American writers such as June Jordan, who has recently championed him as a "white father" whom reactionary college professors in the United States have repressed.

Jordan's view is quite similar in this respect to Hughes's, as his 1946 essay "The Ceaseless Rings of Walt Whitman" makes clear: "Many timid poetry lovers over the years have been frightened away from his *Leaves of Grass* . . . because of his simplicity. Perhaps, too, because his all embracing words lock arms with workers and farmers, Negroes and whites, Asiatics and Europeans, serfs and free men, beaming democracy to all, many academic-minded intellectual isolationists in America have had little use for Whitman, and have impeded his handclasp with today by keeping him imprisoned in silence on library shelves" (96–97). Knowing that Whitman's name had been invoked in movements for social change, Hughes claimed that *Leaves of Grass* had literally helped millions of people struggling against oppression around the world.

North American critics have generally dismissed Latin American inter-pretations of Whitman as naïve, overly politicized, or insufficiently attuned to Whitman's craftsmanship. These dismissals can be attributed not only to the North Americans' more accurate knowledge of the poet's life but also to the ways in which critical trends within the United States have shaped the academic readings of *Leaves of Grass* and to the way in which literature has been institutionalized. In the revaluation of Whitman which coincided with his rising status within English departments, the earlier left-wing, populist, politically engaged, prophetic, and "public" Whitman (espoused by such fig-ures as Eugene Debs, Clarence Darrow, and Emma Goldman when Hughes was young) was debunked along with his disciples, while the private, rela-tively apolitical poet was discovered beneath the yawping pose. Whitman's academic reputation grew as the work of critics such as Gay Wilson Allen, James E. Miller, and Edwin Haviland Miller in the 1950s and 1960s suc-ceeded in differentiating the weaker, supposedly more prophetic verse from the stronger, more aesthetically satisfying "poetry." The interpretive shift contributed significantly to the developing appreciation of Whitman's work but had the effect of devaluing, even suppressing, many of those elements of *Leaves of Grass* which had done most to gain Whitman a broad international following and which had most appealed to Hughes. This may partly account for our difficulty in recognizing the close relationship between Whitman and African-American poetry. Precisely the elements that scholars found in Whitman as they established him in university curricula were the elements Hughes deprecated in other modern poets: linguistic "difficulty" or appar-ently willful obscurity, literary allusiveness, and private confession—quali-ties professors love to explore but that often alienate "common" readers (and that one rarely finds in Hughes's work).

The legendary Whitman Hughes encountered in Latin America was also ubiquitous among writers in Spain during its civil war; Whitman was a heroic personage to such poets as Federico García Lorca and Miguel de Una-muno, not to mention Neruda, who also fought for the antifascist cause. These are all people whom Hughes knew in Spain. García Lorca became one of Hughes's favorite poets; indeed, Hughes translated the play *Bodas de Sangre* and some of the gypsy ballads, and he intended to translate *The Poet in New York* at one point. The "Ode to Walt Whitman" in this book-long poem functions as what one translator calls "a synthesis, climax, and solution to the underlying theme of the book" (Jaen, 81). But what is more intriguing about *The Poet in New York* is the connection it draws between the spirit of Whitman and black American culture. In this poem, black people emerge as those who, still expressing the elemental passions and desires of humanity, hold out the hope of realizing Whitman's dream.

At the end of "Ode to Walt Whitman," Whitman's spirit is to be carried on by a black American child who will "announce to the whites of the gold / the coming of the reign of the wheat," a veiled allusion to *Leaves of Grass* (as quoted in Craige, 79). Indeed, throughout *The Poet in New York,* the suggested revolt of African-Americans against an oppressive, dehumanizing, and mechanistic civilization seems the only hope of realizing the sort of society of which Whitman had dreamed. A host of themes and images interrelate Whitman and the black people of Harlem: the ability to dream (one of Hughes's constant themes), the power of "blood," erotic energy, closeness to nature, water and beach imagery, a valuing of community, and a subversive threat to socio-economic oppression. The "Ode to Whitman" initiates a turn in the poem as a whole toward the speaker's reconnection with nature, accompanied by a growing sense of hope and community. This shift is signified in part by the increasingly musical and incantatory style, which reaches its apogee in the optimistic closing section, "*Son* of the Negroes in Cuba." The poem must have hit Hughes with great force, for he had earlier convinced Nicolás Guillén of Cuba to use folk-based *son* lyrics as a basis for poetry. Of course, by the mid-thirties the main thrust of Hughes's poetry had already been determined, but what I would like to emphasize is an intertextual field connecting Whitman, Hughes, García Lorca, and such Latin American poets as Guillén, a field which considerably alters our vision of "American" poetry and the relationships between its "black" and "white" avatars. As late as 1965, when the separatist Black Arts Movement was gaining steam, Hughes wrote a show called "Tell It to Telstar" in which he combined excerpts from Whitman with songs and spirituals of black America.

The nature and history of Langston Hughes's relationship to Whitman complicate the project of developing sweeping theoretical models for the complex interplay between what at any given time might be constituted as particular radical traditions in the United States, for the centers of these traditions do not hold. Authors are not unitary figures inhabiting fixed cultural coordinates but are often liminal voyagers upon open roads, transgressors of even our latest pieties. This is not necessarily because they were in living fact freer than we give them credit for, nor because of some timeless, transcendent property but because of the subversive, multivalent quality of poetic signification itself, because of the tendency of artists to straddle thresholds of social difference, which may be fundamental to their roles, and because of the multiple ways in which authors have been received on their textual journeys.

Works Cited

Alegría, Fernando. *Walt Whitman en Hispanoamerica.* Mexico City: Ediciones Studium, 1954.

Craige, Betty Jean. *Lorca's* Poet in New York: *The Fall into Consciousness.* Lexington: University of Kentucky Press, 1977.

Grünzweig, Walter. "Whitmania as an Intercultural Phenomenon." *Walt Whitman Quarterly Review* 5(1988): 16–26.

Hughes, Langston. *The Weary Blues.* New York: Knopf, 1926.

———. "The Ceaseless Rings of Walt Whitman." In Perlman, et al.

Hughes, Langston, and Arna Bontemps, eds. *Poetry of the Negro, 1746–1949.* Garden City, NY: Doubleday, 1949.

Jaen, Didier Tisdel, trans and ed. *Homage to Walt Whitman: A Collection of Poems from the Spanish.* Tuscaloosa: University of Alabama, 1969.

Perlman, Jim, Ed Folsom, and Dan Campion, eds. *Walt Whitman: The Measure of His Song.* Minneapolis: Holy Cow! Press, 1981.

Rampersad, Arnold. *The Life of Langston Hughes.* 2 Vols. New York: Oxford, 1986.

Whitman, Walt. *Leaves of Grass: Comprehensive Reader's Edition.* Edited by Harold W. Blodgett and Sculley Bradley. New York: NYU Press, 1965.

Sample Student Research Paper

Grace R. Alston

Professor Hall

African-American Literature

September 15, 1997

Challenging the Father/Challenging the Self:
Langston Hughes's "The Negro Speaks of Rivers."

Langston Hughes's career as a poet began with
the publication of "The Negro Speaks of Rivers"
in the June 1921 issue of The Crisis. Hughes
wrote this poem during a trip to Mexico to visit
his father, African-American businessman James
Hughes. James Hughes, an "unfeeling, domineering,
and materialistic man, scornful of Indians and
blacks and the poor in general, and contemptuous
of his son's gentler pace and artistic temperament" (Rampersad 54), had purposefully removed
himself from African-American life in the United
States. Throughout the trip Langston Hughes
dreaded the confrontation he knew he would have
with his father about his desire to become a
writer. He was very anxious, even depressed, but
as he wrote, "my best poems were all written when
I felt the worst. When I was happy, I didn't
write anything" (Rampersad 54).

Herman Beavers argues that the emotionally
distant relationship between Hughes and his
father influenced the younger Hughes to adopt
"a posture both inside and outside the race" (97).
According to Beavers, Hughes's position inside
the race was to affirm blackness, counter to his

*Background
of poem*

Alston 2

father's racial beliefs. Hughes's position outside the race was to maintain objectivity and
artistic distance while simultaneously displaying
an artist's passion (Beavers 97). Ironically,
then, Hughes's desire to celebrate blackness--
with a kind of passionate objectivity--was born
out of the dysfunctional relationship he had with
his father. In Hughes's case we can see typical
adolescent rebellion connected to the unusual
task of confronting racism. Not only did Hughes
reject his father's feelings about race, but he
also insisted on becoming a writer even though
his father saw writing as impractical and somehow
not quite manly.

How did Hughes suppress such personal experience in his poetry while broadly describing an
entire race without appearing to stereotype? Much
later in his career, Hughes advised other African-
American writers to "step outside yourself, then
look back--and you will see how human, yet how
beautiful and black you are. How very black--even
when you're integrated" (Hughes, "Writers" 41).
The specific form of "The Negro Speaks of Rivers" **Thesis statement**
reveals Hughes's struggle with this double consciousness. In this poem, Hughes actively engages his father's racism, but he also develops
a voice that allows him to do more than just
affirm blackness. The poem also celebrates the
role of African-Americans in the universal human
community.

Alston 3

Hughes understood early in life the peculiarities of this double consciousness, and investigated ways it could be managed in poetry. Hughes understood this concept of "double consciousness" as early as high school; he believed that the role of class poet was thrust upon him at Cleveland's Central High because he was black, and supposed to have "rhythm." The idea that his individuality was not recognized--that he was seen in terms of racial stereotypes--caused him great anxiety, an anxiety heightened by his father's questioning of African-American character. In the face of so much conflict, it is not surprising that "double consciousness" became one of Hughes's poetic themes (Rampersad 54).

In "The Negro Artist and the Racial Mountain" Hughes argues that "white" is the symbol of American standardization (36). Against this burdensome norm, he suggested that the Negro artist would have a high mountain to climb in order to discover the self and the community. Hughes was able to climb this mountain, but at what emotional cost? (If some of Hughes's best poems were written when he felt most pessimistic about the prospects for black people, the number of poems reflecting this pessimism suggests he was frequently under stress.) He was able, however, to transform negative emotions into strong, accessible poems. He experienced great pain while writing "The Negro Speaks of Rivers," but was able to put this emotion aside as he glanced out of a train window

Description of Hughes's experience and understanding of "double consciousness"

Description of the poem's challenge to "double consciousness"

Alston 4

and became mesmerized by the Mississippi River.
As the image of the river engulfed him, he trans-
formed his desire to rebel against his father's
disapproval into a poem that Karen Jackson Ford
notes is uncharacteristic because of its strong
"oratorical tone" (75). In the poem Hughes writes
these lines:

> I've known rivers:
> I've known rivers ancient as the world
>   and older than the flow of human blood
>   in human veins.
>
> My soul has grown deep like the rivers.
>   (1-5)

The words "I've known rivers" are universal--and
ironic given the rest of the poem. The words up-
lift and inspire because they remind us of shared
experience. "Knowing" and "rivers" are not extraordinary; they suggest shared feelings, and in
this sharing we begin a process by which readers
come to appreciate blackness.

Hughes's tone in "The Negro Speaks of Rivers"
is marked by struggle and, despite the poem's
affirmation, by anger (20). The "I" of the poem
says that he has "known rivers ancient as human
blood" and that his "soul has grown deep like the
rivers." (Hughes also once wrote of the time with
his father that "Anger clotted in every vein, and
my tongue tasted like dry blood" [Rampersad 54].)
With this use of blood Hughes identifies a common

Alston 5

human denominator: our biology, or bloodline. The
poem also recalls a time in America wherein if a
person had "one drop" of "Negro blood" he or she
was not entitled to full citizenship. The separateness Hughes felt as an American was the same
separateness he felt as a son. The "bloodline"
was their only tie.

Analysis of poetic
tone and its
relationship to
Hughes's goal

In focusing on the following lines, Karen
Jackson Ford suggests the poem's "mythic scope"
(75):

> I bathed in the Euphrates when dawns were
> young.
> I built my hut near the Congo and it
> lulled me to sleep.
> I looked upon the Nile and raised the
> pyramids above it.
> I heard the singing of the Mississippi
> when Abe Lincoln went down to New
> Orleans, and I've seen its muddy bosom
> turn all golden in the sunset.
>
> I've known rivers:
> Ancient dusky rivers.
>
> My soul has grown deep like the rivers.
> (5-13)

The scope here is perhaps as much historic as
mythic. Although Hughes depicts certain conventions of black culture in an imaginative and
symbolic way, his choice of rivers suggests

Analysis of historical
and geographical
allusions and their
relationship to
Hughes's goals

a very particular history. The Congo and Nile
illustrate the beauty of blackness and its accomplishments; they appear "naturally" alongside
the Euphrates, and with it suggest the beginnings
of civilization. In this way, Hughes makes clear
to his father--and to the nation--the nobility of
an African past. Moreover, his invocation of the
Mississippi not only places the American river
in a continuous historical relationship with the
Euphrates but also introduces the question of
slavery. Once again, Hughes is able to perform
the double task of confronting both American
culture and his father. The image of defenseless
slaves being sold up and down the Mississippi
River's "muddy bosom" may have reminded him of
his own defenseless position in his relationship
with his father. And as the "muddy bosom" turning "golden in the sunset" suggests freedom for
slaves, it may have also meant for Hughes freedom
from his father.

Repetition also contributes to the poem's effect. Because the poem promotes healing and liberation, Hughes uses words implying motion, such
as "built," "bathed," "looked," "raised," and
"singing," emphasizing ritual and religion.
"Rivers," of course, works in a slightly different manner, but it may be the most effective
means by which Hughes communicates his feeling
of displacement. Like a kind of chant, creation
of this complex rhythm is the most striking way
he rises to his double challenge, but the success

Alston 7

of this "rhythm" is based in readers' collective experience, and not upon racial stereotype.

Hughes believed that black writers had a responsibility to reveal to whites that blacks could do more than sing, dance, laugh, and make music. He believed black writers had a role to play in racial reconciliation (Hughes, "To Negro Writers" 41), and his ability to affirm blackness without stereotyping is what earns him his distinction as a poet. That the impetus for his racial affirmations came, at least partially, from his troubled relationship with his father is striking. His passion for "blackness" increased as he resisted his black father, while his ability to develop a poetic persona emerged from his awareness of his own "double position."

Conclusion with restatement of thesis

Works Cited

Beavers, Herman. "Dead Rocks and Sleeping Men:
    Aurality in the Aesthetic of Langston
    Hughes." Hall 97-103.

Ford, Karen Jackson. "Do Right to Write Right:
    Langston Hughes's Aesthetics of Simplicity."
    Hall 75-97.

Hall, James C., ed. <u>Langston Hughes: A Collection
    of Poems</u>. The Harcourt Brace Casebook Series
    in Literature: Fort Worth: Harcourt, 1998.

Hughes, Langston. "The Negro Artist and the
    Racial Mountain." Hall 36-40.

---. "The Negro Speaks of Rivers." Hall 20.

---. "To Negro Writers." Hall 41-42.

Rampersad, Arnold. "The Origins of Poetry in
    Langston Hughes." Hall 54-65.

Bibliography

This bibliography is selective. It does not include secondary work on Hughes's drama, fiction, autobiographies, or children's books unless that work includes significant commentary on the poetry. Neither does the bibliography include book reviews. One comprehensive bibliography is Thomas A. Mikolzyk, *Langston Hughes: A Bio-Bibliography* (New York: Greenwood Press, 1990). For reviews, in particular, see Tish Dace, *Langston Hughes: The Contemporary Reviews* (New York: Cambridge University Press, 1997). Students should note that there is a scholarly journal specifically devoted to the exploration and criticism of Hughes's work: *The Langston Hughes Review.* Other important journals which focus on African-American literature include *Callaloo, African-American Review,* and *Obsidian.*

Works by Langston Hughes

ANTHOLOGIES

Hughes, Langston, and Arna Bontemps. *The Poetry of the Negro, 1746–1949.* New York: Doubleday, 1949.
———. *The Book of Negro Folklore.* New York: Dodd, 1958.

AUTOBIOGRAPHY

Hughes, Langston. *The Big Sea.* New York: Knopf, 1940.
———. *I Wonder as I Wander.* New York: Knopf, 1956.

CORRESPONDENCE

Nichols, Charles H., ed. *Arna Bontemps and Langston Hughes: Letters 1925–1967.* New York: Dodd, 1977.

DRAMA

Hughes, Langston. *Five Plays*. Bloomington, IN: Indiana UP, 1968.
———, and Zora Neale Hurston. *Mule Bone*. New York: HarperPerennial, 1991.

ESSAYS, JOURNALISM

DeSantis, Christopher C., ed. *Langston Hughes and the Chicago Defender: Essays on Race, Politics, and Culture, 1942–62*. Urbana: U of Illinois P, 1995.

FICTION

Hughes, Langston. *Not Without Laughter*. New York: Knopf, 1930.
———. *The Ways of White Folks*. New York: Knopf, 1933.
———, and Roy DeCarava. *Sweet Flypaper of Life*. New York: Simon, 1955.
Harper, Akiba Sullivan, ed. *Not So Simple: The "Simple" Stories by Langston Hughes*. Columbia: U of Missouri P, 1995.
———. *The Short Stories of Langston Hughes*. New York: Hill, 1996.

MISCELLANEOUS

Hughes, Langston. *The Langston Hughes Reader*. New York: Braziller, 1958.

POETRY

Langston Hughes. *The Weary Blues*. New York: Knopf, 1926.
———. *Fine Clothes to the Jew*. New York: Knopf, 1927.
———. *The Negro Mother and Other Dramatic Recitations*. New York: Golden Stair, 1931.
———. *The Dream Keeper and Other Poems*. New York: Knopf, 1932.
———. *Scottsboro Limited*. New York: Golden Stair, 1932.
———. *A New Song*. New York: International Workers Order, 1938.
———. *Shakespeare in Harlem*. New York: Knopf, 1942.
———. *Freedom's Plow*. New York: Musette, 1943.
———. *Jim Crow's Last Stand*. Atlanta, GA: Negro Publication Society of America, 1943.
———. *Fields of Wonder*. New York: Knopf, 1947.
———. *One-Way Ticket*. New York: Knopf, 1949.
———. *Montage of a Dream Deferred*. New York: Henry Holt, 1951.
———. *Selected Poems*. New York: Knopf, 1959.
———. *Ask Your Mama: Twelve Moods for Jazz*. New York: Knopf, 1961.

————. *The Panther and the Lash.* New York: Knopf, 1967.

Rampersad, Arnold, and David Roessel, eds. *Collected Poems of Langston Hughes.* New York: Vintage, 1994.

POLITICAL WRITINGS

Berry, Faith. *Good Morning Revolution: Uncollected Writings of Social Protest by Langston Hughes.* New York: Citadel, 1992.

TRANSLATIONS

Hughes, Langston. "Gypsy Ballads." Ed. Federico García Lorca. *Beloit Poetry Journal* (Fall 1952).

————. *Selected Poems of Gabriela Mistral.* Bloomington: Indiana UP, 1957.

Reference

Chapman, Dorothy. *Index to Black Poetry.* Boston: G. K. Hall, 1974.

Dace, Tish. *Langston Hughes: The Contemporary Reviews.* New York: Cambridge UP, 1997.

Etheridge, Sharynn O. "Langston Hughes: An Annotated Bibliography (1977–1986)." *Langston Hughes Review* 11.1 (1992):41–57.

Mandelik, Peter, and Stanley Schatt. *A Concordance to the Poetry of Langston Hughes.* Detroit: Gale Research, 1975.

Miller, R. Baxter. *Langston Hughes and Gwendolyn Brooks: A Reference Guide.* Boston: G. K. Hall, 1978.

Biography

Berry, Faith. *Langston Hughes: Before and Beyond Harlem.* Westport, CT: Lawrence Hill, 1983.

Hurst, Catherine Daniels. "Langston Hughes." *Dictionary of Literary Biography.* Vol. 7. Detroit: Gale Research, 1981.

Meltzer, Milton. *Langston Hughes: A Biography.* New York: Crowell, 1968.

Rampersad, Arnold. *The Life of Langston Hughes, 1902–1967.* 2 Vols. New York: Oxford UP, 1986–88.

General Criticism

Ako, Edward O. "Langston Hughes and the Negritude Movement: A Study in Literary Influence." *CLA Journal* 28 (1983–4):46–56.

Asgill, Eddie Omotayo. "Langston Hughes and Africa." In *Of Dreams Deferred, Dead or Alive: African Perspectives on African-American Writers*, ed. Femi Ojo-Ade, 43–52. Westport, CT: Greenwood Press, 1996.

Barksdale, Richard K. *Langston Hughes: The Poet and His Critics.* Chicago: American Library Association, 1977.

Berry, Faith. "The Universality of Langston Hughes." *The Langston Hughes Review* 1.2 (1982):1–10.

Bloom, Harold, ed. *Langston Hughes.* New York: Chelsea House, 1989.

Bogumil, Mary L., and Michael R. Molino. "Pretext, Context, Subtext: Textual Power in the Writing of Langston Hughes, Richard Wright, and Martin Luther King, Jr." *College English* 52.7 (Nov. 1990):800–11.

Borden, Anne. "Heroic 'Hussies' and 'Brilliant Queers': Genderracial Resistance in the Works of Langston Hughes." *African-American Review* 28.3 (1994): 333–45.

Chinitz, David. "Rejuvenation Through Joy: Langston Hughes, Primitivism, and Jazz." *American Literary History* 9.1 (1997):60–81.

Chioni Moore, David. "Local Color, Global 'Color': Langston Hughes, the Black Atlantic, and Soviet Central Asia, 1932." *Research in African Literatures* 27.4 (1996):49–70.

Chrisman, Robert. "Nicolás Guillén, Langston Hughes, and the Black American/ Afro-Cuban Connection." *Michigan Quarterly Review* 33.4 (1994):807–20.

Cobb, Martha K. "Concepts of Blackness in the Poetry of Nicolás Guillén, Jacques Roumain, and Langston Hughes." *CLA Journal* 18 (1974–75): 262–72.

———. *Harlem, Haiti, and Havana: A Comparative Critical Study of Langston Hughes, Jacques Roumain, and Nicolás Guillén.* Washington, DC: Three Continents Press, 1979.

Cullen, Countee. "Poet on Poet." *Opportunity* 4 (March 1926):73.

Dace, Tish. "On Langston Hughes: Poet." *American Poetry Review* 24.6 (Nov.– Dec. 1995):35–38.

Davis, Arthur P. "Langston Hughes." In *From the Dark Tower.* Washington, DC: Howard University Press, 1974.

Deck, Alice A. "Introduction: Langston Hughes and the African Diaspora." *The Langston Hughes Review* 5.1 (1986):iv–vi.

DeSantis, Christopher. "Rage, Repudiation, and Endurance: Langston Hughes's Radical Writings." *Langston Hughes Review* 12.1 (1993):31–9.

Dixon, Melvin. "Rivers Remembering Their Source: Comparative Studies in Black Literary History—Langston Hughes, Jacques Romain, and Negritude." In

Afro-American Literature: The Reconstruction of Instruction, ed. Dexter Fisher and Robert B. Stepto. New York: Modern Language Association, 1979.

Emanuel, James A. *Langston Hughes.* New York: Twayne, 1967.

Fowler, Carolyn. "The Shared Vision of Langston Hughes and Jacques Roumain." *Black American Literature Forum* 15 (1983):84–88.

Garner, Thomas, and Carolyn Calloway-Thomas. "Langston Hughes's Message for the Black Masses." *Communication Quarterly* 39 (1991):164–78.

Gates, Henry Louis, Jr. "The Hungry Icon: Langston Hughes Rides a Blue Note." *Village Voice Literary Supplement* (July 1989):8–13.

Govan, Sandra Y. "Kindred Spirits and Sympathetic Souls: Langston Hughes and Gwendolyn Bennett in the Harlem Renaissance." In *Langston Hughes: The Man, His Art, and His Continuing Influence,* ed. C. James Trotman. New York: Garland, 1995. 75–85.

Gresson, Aaron D. "Beyond Selves Deferred: Langston Hughes's Style and the Psychology of Black Selfhood." *Langston Hughes Review* 4.1 (1985):47–54.

Holmes, Eugene C. "Langston Hughes: Philosopher Poet." *Freedomways* 8 (1968):144–51.

Jackson, Blyden. "Claude McKay and Langston Hughes: The Harlem Renaissance and More." *Pembroke Magazine* 6 (1975):43–8.

———. "Renaissance in the Twenties." In *The Twenties: Fiction, Poetry, Drama,* ed. Warren French. Deland, FL: Everett/Edwards, 1975.

Jackson, Richard. "Langston Hughes and the African Diaspora in South America." *The Langston Hughes Review* 5.1 (1986):23–33.

———. "The Shared Vision of Langston Hughes and Black Hispanic Writers." *Black American Literature Forum* 15.3 (1981):89–92.

Johnson, Patricia A. and Walter C. Farrell. "How Langston Hughes Used the Blues." *MELUS* 6 (1979):55–63.

Kent, George E. "Langston Hughes and Afro-American Folk and Cultural Tradition." In *Blackness and the Adventure of Western Culture.* Chicago: Third World Press, 1972.

Lubin, Maurice A. "Langston Hughes and Haiti." *The Langston Hughes Review* 6.1 (1987):4–7.

Martin, Dellita L. "Langston Hughes's Use of the Blues." *CLA Journal* 22 (1978–79):151–59.

Martin-Ogunsola, Dellita L. "Langston Hughes and the Musico-Poetry of African Diaspora." *The Langston Hughes Review* 5.1 (1986):1–17.

Miller, R. Baxter. *The Art and Imagination of Langston Hughes.* Lexington, KY: UP of Kentucky, 1989.

Moses, Wilson Jeremiah. "More Stately Mansions: New Negro Movements and Langston Hughes's Literary Theory." *Langston Hughes Review* 4.1 (1985): 40–6.

Mullen, Edward J. *Langston Hughes in the Hispanic World and Haiti.* Hamden, CT: Arcon, 1977.

————. "Langston Hughes in Mexico and Cuba." *Review: Latin American Literature and Arts* 47 (1993):23–7.

————. "Langston Hughes and the Development of Afro-Hispanic Literature: Diasporan Connections." *Black Scholar* 26.2 (1996):10.

————, ed. *Critical Essays on Langston Hughes.* Boston: G. K. Hall, 1986.

Neal, Larry. "Langston Hughes: Black America's Poet Laureate." In *American Writing Today,* ed. Richard Kostelanetz. Troy, NY: Whitson, 1991.

O'Daniel, Therman B. "Lincoln's Man of Letters." *Lincoln University Bulletin* (July 1964):9–12.

————, ed. *Langston Hughes, Black Genius: A Critical Evaluation.* New York: William Morrow, 1971.

Peidra, Jose. "Through Blues." In *Do the Americas Have a Common Literature?* ed. Gustavo Perez Firmat. Durham, NC: Duke UP, 1990.

Presley, James. "Langston Hughes: A Personal Farewell." *Southwest Review* 54 (1969):79–84.

Prowle, Allen D. "Langston Hughes." In *The Black American Writer* Vol. 2, *Poetry and Drama.* Ed. C. W. E. Bigsby. Deland, FL: Everett/ Edwards, 1969.

Rampersad, Arnold. "The Origins of Poetry in Langston Hughes." *Southern Review* 21 (1985):695–705.

————. "The Universal and the Particular in Afro-American Poetry." *CLA Journal* 15.1 (September 1981):1–17.

————. "Langston Hughes and Approaches to Modernism in the Harlem Renaissance." In *The Harlem Renaissance: Revaluations,* ed. Amritjit Singh, et al., 49–71. New York: Garland, 1989.

Singh, Armritjit. "Beyond the Mountain: Langston Hughes on Race/Class and Art." *The Langston Hughes Review* 6.1 (1987):37–43.

Sundquist, Eric J. "Who Was Langston Hughes?" *Commentary* 102.6 (1996): 55–59.

Tracy, Steven C. *Langston Hughes and the Blues.* Urbana, IL: U of Illinois P, 1988.

Trotman, James C., ed. *Langston Hughes: The Man, His Art, and His Continuing Influence.* New York: Garland, 1995.

Vendler, Helen. "The Unweary Blues." *The New Republic* 212.10 (March 1995): 37–42.

Walker, Alice. "Turning Into Love: Some Thoughts on Surviving and Meeting Langston Hughes." *Callaloo* 12 (1989):663–66.

Wall, Cheryl A. "Whose Sweet Angel Child? Blues Women, Langston Hughes, and Writing During the Harlem Renaissance." In *Langston Hughes: The Man, His Art, and His Continuing Influence,* ed. C. James Trotman. New York: Garland, 1995. 37–50.

Williams, Sherley Anne. "Langston Hughes and the Negro Renaissance." *Langston Hughes Review* 4.1 (1985):37–9.

Winz, Cary D. "Langston Hughes: A Kansas Poet in the Harlem Renaissance." *Kansas Quarterly* 7 (1975):58–71.

Criticism of Hughes's Poetry

Barksdale, Richard. "Comic Relief in Langston Hughes's Poetry." *Black American Literature Forum* 15.3 (1981):108–11.

———. "Langston Hughes and the Blues He Couldn't Lose." In *The Harlem Renaissance: Reevaluations,* ed. Amritjit Singh, et al. New York: Garland, 1989.

Beyer, William C. "A Certain Kind of Aesthete: Langston Hughes's *Shakespeare in Harlem.*" In *A Humanist's Legacy: Essays in Honor of John Christian Bale,* ed. Dennis M. Jones. Decorah, IA: Luther College, 1990.

Blake, Susan L. "The American Dream and the Legacy of Revolution in the Poetry of Langston Hughes." *Black American Literature Forum* 14 (1980): 100–04.

Bonner, Patricia E. "Cryin' the Jazzy Blues and Livin' Blue Jazz: Analyzing the Blues and Jazz Poetry of Langston Hughes." *West Georgia College Review* 20 (May 1990):15–28.

Brown, Lloyd W. "The Portrait of the Artist as a Black American in the Poetry of Langston Hughes." *Studies in Black Literature* (1974):24–27.

Cartey, Wilfred. "Four Shadows of Harlem." *Negro Digest* 18 (August 1969): 22–25, 83–92.

Chinitz, David. "Literacy and Authenticity: The Blues Poems of Langston Hughes." *Callaloo* 19.1 (1996):177–93.

Cobb, Martha. "Langston Hughes: The Writer, His Poetics, and the Artistic Process." *Langston Hughes Review* 2.2 (1983):1–5.

Culp, Mary. "Religion in the Poetry of Langston Hughes." *Phylon* 48.3 (1987): 240–45.

Davis, Arthur P. "The Harlem of Langston Hughes's Poetry." *Phylon* 13.4 (1952): 276–83.

———. "The Tragic Mulatto Theme in Six Works of Langston Hughes." *Phylon* 16.2 (1955): 195–204.

———. "Langston Hughes: Cool Poet." *CLA Journal* 11 (1967–68):280–96.

Diaz-Diacaretz, Myriam. "Society (Pro)poses and Madam (Dis)poses." *The Langston Hughes Review* 6.1 (1987):30–36.

Emanuel, James A. "The Literary Experiments of Langston Hughes." *CLA Journal* (June 1968):335–44.

Ensslen, Klaus. "Plain Living and Plain Talk in Langston Hughes's 'Mother to Son': A Poetics of the Black Folk Voice." *Anglistik & Englischunterricht* 53 (1994):87–96.

Farrell, Walter C., Jr., and Patricia A. Johnson. "Poetic Interpretations of Urban Black Folk Culture: Langston Hughes and the 'Bebop' Era." *MELUS* 8.3 (1981):57–73.

———. "How Langston Hughes Used the Blues." *MELUS* 6 (1979):55–63.

———. "The Jazz Poetry of Langston Hughes." *Minority Voices* 4.1 (1980):11–21.

Ferrell, Tracy J. Prince. "'Theme for English B' and the Dreams of Langston Hughes." *English Review* 6.1 (September 1995):36–7.

Garber, Earlene D. "Form as a Complement to Content in Three of Langston Hughes's Poems." *Negro American Literature Forum* 5 (1971):137–39.

Hansell, William H. "Black Music in the Poetry of Langston Hughes: Roots, Race, Release." *Obsidian* 4 (1978):16–38.

Hernton, Calvin. "The Poetic Consciousness of Langston Hughes: From Affirmation to Revolution." *Langston Hughes Review* 12.1 (1993):2–9.

Hoagwood, Kimberly. "Two States of Mind in Dream Variations." *The Langston Hughes Review* 2.2 (1983):16–18.

Hudson, Theodore. "Technical Aspects of the Poetry of Langston Hughes." *Black World* 22 (1973):24–25.

Jackson, Blyden. "From One 'New Negro' to Another." In *Black Poetry in America: Two Essays on Historical Interpretation.* Baton Rouge, LA: Louisiana State UP, 1974.

Jarroway, David R. "Montage of an Otherness Deferred: Dreaming Subjectivity in Langston Hughes." *American Literature* 68.4 (December 1996):819–41.

Jemie, Onwuchekwa. *Langston Hughes: An Introduction to the Poetry.* New York: Columbia UP, 1976.

Martin, Dellita L. "The 'Madame Poems' as Dramatic Monologue." *Black American Literature Forum* 15 (1981):97–99.

Miller, R. Baxter. "'A Mere Poem': 'Daybreak in Alabama,' A Resolution to Langston Hughes's Theme of Music and Art." *Obsidian* 2 (1976):30–37.

———. "'No Crystal Stair': Unity, Archetype and Symbol in Langston Hughes's Poems on Women." *Negro American Literature Forum* 9 (1975):109–114.

———. "Framing and Framed Languages in Hughes's *Ask Your Mama: 12 Moods for Jazz." MELUS* 17.4 (1991–92):3–13.

Ogunyemi, C.O. "In Praise of Things Black: Langston Hughes and Oko p' Bitek." *Contemporary Poetry* 4.1 (1981):19–39.

Peters, Erskine. "Manipulation and Instrument Simulation in *Montage of A Dream Deferred," The Literary Griot* 5.1 (1993):33–49.

Reid, Margaret A. "Langston Hughes: Rhetoric and Protest." *Langston Hughes Review* 3.1 (1984):13–20.

Reini-Grandell, Lynette. "Langston Hughes's Invocation of the Blues and Jazz Tradition Under the Double-Edged Sword of Primitivism." *West Virginia University Philological Papers* 38 (1992):113–23.

Schatt, Stanley. "Langston Hughes: The Minstrel as Artificer." *Journal of Modern Literature* 4 (September 1974):115–20.

Shoptaw, John. "Lyric Incorporated: The Serial Object of George Oppen and Langston Hughes." *Sagetrieb* 12.3 (1993):105–24.

Smith, Raymond. "Langston Hughes: Evolution of the Poetic Persona." *Studies in the Literary Imagination* 7 (1974):49–64.

Spicer, Eloise Y. "The Blues and the Son: Reflections of Black Self-Assertion in the Poetry of Langston Hughes and Nicolás Guillén." *Langston Hughes Review* 3.1 (1984):1–12.

Sweet, Donald. "Langston Hughes's "Hope"." *Langston Hughes Review* 2.2 (1983): 19–21.

Thurston, Michael. "Black Christ, Red Flag: Langston Hughes on Scottsboro." *College Literature* 22.3 (1995):30–49.

Tracy, Steven C. "'Midnight Ruffles of Cat-Gut Lace': The Boogie Poems of Langston Hughes." *College Language Association Journal* 32.1 (1988):55–68.

———. "To the Time of Those Weary Blues: The Influence of the Blues Tradition in Langston Hughes's Blues Poems." *MELUS* 8.3 (1981): 73–98.

———. "Langston Hughes: Poetry, Blues, and Gospel—Somewhere to Stand." In *Langston Hughes: The Man, His Art, and His Continuing Influence,* ed. C. James Trotman. New York: Garland, 1995. 51–61.

Waldron, Edward E. "The Blues Poetry of Langston Hughes." *Negro American Literature Forum* 5 (1971):140–49.

General African-American Literary and Cultural History

Andrews, William L. *The Oxford Companion to African-American Literature.* New York: Oxford, 1997.

Baker, Houston A., Jr. *Long Black Song.* Charlottesville, VA: UP of Virginia, 1972.

———. *Blues, Ideology and Afro-American Literature.* Chicago: U of Chicago P, 1984.

———. *Modernism and the Harlem Renaissance.* Chicago, IL: U of Chicago P, 1987.

Barlow, William. *"Looking Up at Down:" The Emergence of Blues Culture.* Philadelphia: Temple UP, 1989.

Berry, Mary Frances, and John W. Blassingame. *Long Memory: The Black Experience in America.* New York: Oxford, 1982.

Bruce, Dickson. *Black American Writing From the Nadir: The Evolution of A Literary Tradition, 1877–1915.* Baton Rouge, LA: Louisiana State UP, 1989.

Cooke, Michael G. *Afro-American Literature in the Twentieth Century: The Achievement of Intimacy.* New Haven, CT: Yale UP, 1984.

Ellison, Ralph. *Shadow and Act.* New York: Vintage, 1964.

Gates, Henry Louis, Jr. *The Signifying Monkey: A Theory of African-American Literary Criticism.* New York: Oxford, 1987.

Gayle, Addison, ed. *The Black Aesthetic.* Garden City, NY: Doubleday-Anchor, 1972.

Huggins, Nathan. *The Harlem Renaissance.* New York: Oxford, 1971.

Hutchinson, George. *The Harlem Renaissance in Black and White.* Cambridge, MA: Harvard UP, 1995.

Jahn, Janheinz. *MUNTU: An Outline of the New African Culture.* New York: Grove, 1961.

Johnson, Abby Arthur, and Ronald Maberry Johnson. *Propaganda and Aesthetics: The Literary Politics of Afro-American Magazines in the Twentieth Century.* Amherst, MA: U of Massachusetts P, 1979.

Jones, Leroi. *Blues People.* New York: Quill, 1962.

Lewis, David Levering. *When Harlem Was In Vogue.* New York: Knopf, 1981.

Locke, Alain, ed. *The New Negro.* New York: Atheneum, 1968.

Miller, James. "African-American Writing of the 1930s: A Prologue." In *Radical Revisions: Rereading 1930s Culture,* ed. Bill Mullen and Sherry Lee Linkon. Urbana, IL: U of Illinois P, 1996.

Mitchell, Angelyn, ed. *Within the Circle: An Anthology of African-American Literary Criticism from the Harlem Renaissance to the Present.* Durham, NC: Duke UP, 1994.

Murray, Albert. *Stomping the Blues.* New York: McGraw-Hill, 1976.

Powell, Richard J. *Black Art and Culture in the Twentieth Century.* New York: Thames and Hudson, 1997.

Redding, Saunders. *To Make a Poet Black.* Chapel Hill, NC: U of North Carolina P, 1939.

Redmond, Eugene. *Drumvoices: The Mission of Afro-American Poetry.* Garden City, NY: Anchor Books, 1976.

Southern, Eileen. *The Music of Black Americans.* 3rd ed. New York: Norton, 1997.

Stuckey, Sterling. *Going Through the Storm: The Influence of African-American Art on History.* New York: Oxford, 1994.

Wagner, Jean. *Black Poets of the United States: From Paul Laurence Dunbar to Langston Hughes.* Urbana, IL: U of Illinois P, 1973.

African-American Poetry Anthologies

Garrett, Beatrice. *A Bite of Black History.* Los Angeles: Bosck House, 1992.

Gilyard, Keith. *Spirit and Flame: An Anthology of Contemporary African American Poetry.* Syracuse, NY: Syracuse UP, 1997.

Harper, Michael and Anthony Walton, *Every Shut Eye Ain't Asleep: An Anthology of Poetry by African Americans Since 1945.* New York: Little, Brown, 1994.

Jackson, Bruce. *Get Your Ass in the Water and Swim Like Me: Narrative Poetry From Black Oral Tradition.* Cambridge, MA: Harvard UP, 1974.

Major, Clarence. *The Garden Thrives: Twentieth Century African American Poetry.* New York: HarperPerennial, 1996.

Miller, E. Ethelbert. *In Search of Color Everywhere: A Collection of African American Poetry.* New York: Stewart, Tabori, and Chang, 1994.

Randall, Dudley. *The Black Poets.* New York: Bantam, 1971.

Saint, Assoto. *Here to Dare: 10 Gay Black Poets.* New York: Galliens, 1992.

Sherman, Joan. *Collected Black Women's Poetry.* New York: Oxford, 1988.

———. *African-American Poetry of the Nineteenth-Century: An Anthology.* Urbana, IL: U of Illinois P, 1992.

Spears, Alan. *Fast Talk, Full Volume: An Anthology of Contemporary African-American Poetry.* Cabin John, MD: Gut Punch Press, 1993.

Stetson, Erlene. *Black Sister: Poetry by Black American Women, 1746–1980.* Bloomington, IN: Indiana UP, 1980.

Ward, Jerry. *Trouble the Water: 250 Years of African-American Poetry.* New York: Mentor, 1997.

Wolfe, Charles K., ed. *Thomas Talley's Negro Folk Rhymes.* Knoxville, TN: U of Tennessee P, 1991.

Audio-Visual Resources

FILM AND VIDEO

Langston Hughes. Videocassette. American School Publishers, 1990.

Langston Hughes. Videocassette. Encyclopedia Britannica, 1994.

Langston Hughes: The Dream Keeper. Dir. St. Clair Bourne. Videocassette. Mystic Fire Video, 1995.

Langston Hughes: Poet. Dir. Amy Tiehel. Videocassette. Schlessinger Video, n.d.

Langston Hughes: The Poet in Our Hearts. Videocassette. Chip Taylor Communications, 1994.

Looking for Langston. Dir. Isaac Julien. Videocassette. Water Bearer Films, 1992.

Voices and Visions, Part 3: Langston Hughes. Prod. Jill Janows, et al. Videocassette. New York Center for Visual History, n.d.

SOUND RECORDINGS

Anthology of Negro Poetry. Ed. Arna Bontemps. LP. Folkways Recordings [FL9791], 1954.

Dream Keeper and Other Poems. LP. Folkways [FP 104], 1955.

Langston Hughes: Blues Poet. Interview with Walter Kerr. Audiocassette. n.p.: Center for Cassette Studies.

Langston Hughes Reads. Audiocassette. Caedmon, 1992.
Poetry and Reflections: Langston Hughes. Audiocassette. Caedmon [CDL 51640], 1980.
Sterling Brown & Langston Hughes. Audiocassette. Smithsonian Folkways, 1991.
The Voice of Langston Hughes: Selected Poetry and Prose Read by the Author. Smithsonian Folkways, 1995.
Weary Blues. Verve, 1990.

Internet Resources

African-American Cultural and Literary Web Pages <http://qqq.uls.pvt.k12.mi.us/afamlit.html>.
African-American Mosaic: Library of Congress Study Guide for the Study of Black History and Culture. <http://www.cweb.loc.gov/exhibits/african/intro.html>.
Amistad Research Center <http://www.arc.tulane.edu>.
Crossroads Project: African-American Studies <http://www.georgetown.edu/crossroads/asw/race.html#afr>.
Paul Robeson Library Info Guide: African-American Literature <http://www.libraries.rutgers.edu/rulib/abtlib/camlib/afriamwr.html>.
Resources for Africa and African-American Studies. <http://www.library.vanderbilt.edu/central/afam.html>.

Appendix:
Documenting Sources

A Guide to MLA
Documentation Style

Documentation is the acknowledgment of information from an outside source that you use in a paper. In general, you should give credit to your sources whenever you quote, paraphrase, summarize, or in any other way incorporate borrowed information or ideas into your work. Not to do so—on purpose or by accident—is to commit **plagiarism,** to appropriate the intellectual property of others. By following accepted conventions of documentation, you not only help avoid plagiarism, but also show your readers that you write with care and precision. In addition, you enable them to distinguish your ideas from those of your sources and, if they wish, to locate and consult the sources you cite.

Not all ideas from your sources need to be documented. You can assume that certain information—facts from encyclopedias, textbooks, newspapers, magazines, and dictionaries, or even from television and radio—is common knowledge. Even if the information is new to you, it need not be documented as long as it is found in several reference sources and as long as you do not use the exact wording of your source. Information that is in dispute or that is the original contribution of a particular person, however, *must* be documented. You need not, for example, document the fact that Arthur Miller's *Death of a Salesman* was first performed in 1949 or that it won a Pulitzer Prize for drama. (You could find this information in any current encyclopedia.) You would, however, have to document a critic's interpretation of a performance or a scholar's analysis of an early draft of the play, even if you do not use your source's exact words.

Students of literature use the documentation style recommended by the Modern Language Association of America (MLA), a professional organization of more than twenty-five thousand teachers and students of English and other languages. This method of documentation, the one that you should use any time you write a literature paper, has three components: *parenthetical references in the text, a list of works cited,* and *explanatory notes.*

Parenthetical References in the Text

MLA documentation uses references inserted in parentheses within the text that refer to an alphabetical list of works cited at the end of the paper. A typical **parenthetical reference** consists of the author's last name and a page number.

> Gwendolyn Brooks uses the sonnet form to create poems that have a wide social and aesthetic range (Williams 972).

If you use more than one source by the same author, include a shortened title in the parenthetical reference. In the following entry, "Brooks's Way" is a shortened form of the complete title of the article "Gwendolyn Brooks's Way with the Sonnet."

> Brooks not only knows Shakespeare, Spenser, and Milton, but she also knows the full range of African-American poetry (Williams, "Brooks's Way" 972).

If you mention the author's name or the title of the work in your paper, only a page reference is necessary.

> According to Gladys Margaret Williams in "Gwendolyn Brooks's Way with the Sonnet," Brooks combines a sensitivity to poetic forms with a depth of emotion appropriate for her subject matter (972–73).

Keep in mind that you use different punctuation for parenthetical references used with *paraphrases and summaries,* with *direct quotations run in with the text,* and with *quotations of more than four lines.*

Paraphrases and Summaries

Place the parenthetical reference after the last word of the sentence and before the final punctuation:

> In her works Brooks combines the pessimism of Modernist poetry with the optimism of the Harlem Renaissance (Smith 978).

Direct quotations run in with the text

Place the parenthetical reference after the quotation marks and before the final punctuation:

> According to Gary Smith, Brooks's <u>A Street in Bronzeville</u> "conveys the primacy of suffering in the lives of poor Black women" (980).

> According to Gary Smith, the poems in <u>A Street in Bronzeville</u>, "served notice that Brooks had learned her craft . . ." (978).

> Along with Thompson we must ask, "Why did it take so long for critics to acknowledge that Gwendolyn Brooks is an important voice in twentieth-century American poetry?" (123)

Quotations set off from the text

Omit the quotation marks and place the parenthetical reference one space after the final punctuation.

> For Gary Smith, the identity of Brooks's African-American women is inextricably linked with their sense of race and poverty:
>
>> For Brooks, unlike the Renaissance poets, the victimization of poor Black women becomes not simply a minor chord but a predominant theme of <u>A Street in Bronzeville</u>. Few, if any, of her female characters are able to free themselves from a web of poverty that threatens to strangle their lives. (980)

[Quotations of more than four lines are indented ten spaces (or one inch) from the margin and are not enclosed within quotation marks. The first line of a single paragraph of quoted material is not indented farther. If you quote two or more paragraphs, indent the first line of each paragraph three additional spaces (one-quarter inch).]

SAMPLE REFERENCES

The following formats are used for parenthetical references to various kinds of sources used in papers about literature. (Keep in mind that the parenthetical reference contains just enough information to enable readers to find the source in the list of works cited at the end of the paper.)

An entire work

August Wilson's play <u>Fences</u> treats many themes frequently expressed in modern drama.

[When citing an entire work, state the name of the author in your paper instead of in a parenthetical reference.]

A work by two or three authors

Myths cut across boundaries and cultural spheres and reappear in strikingly similar forms from country to country (Feldman and Richardson 124).

The effect of a work of literature depends on the audience's predispositions that derive from membership in various social groups (Hovland, Janis, and Kelley 87).

A work by more than three authors

Hawthorne's short stories frequently use a combination of allegorical and symbolic methods (Guerin et al. 91).

[The abbreviation *et al.* is Latin for "and others."]

A work in an anthology

In his essay "Flat and Round Characters" E. M. Forster distinguishes between one-dimensional characters and those that are well developed (Stevick 223–31).

[The parenthetical reference cites the anthology (edited by Stevick) that contains Forster's essay; full information about the anthology appears in the list of works cited.]

A work with volume and page numbers

```
In 1961 one of Albee's plays, The Zoo Story, was
finally performed in America (Eagleton 2:17).
```

An indirect source

```
Wagner observed that myth and history stood before
him "with opposing claims" (qtd. in Winkler 10).
```

[The abbreviation *qtd. in* (quoted in) indicates that the quoted material was not taken from the original source.]

A play or poem with numbered lines

```
"Give thy thoughts no tongue," says Polonius,
"Nor any unproportioned thought his act"
(Ham. 1.3.59-60).
```

[The parentheses contain the act, scene, and line numbers, separated by periods. When included in parenthetical references, titles of the books of the Bible and well-known literary works are often abbreviated—*Gen.* for *Genesis* and *Ado* for *Much Ado about Nothing,* for example.]

```
"I muse my life-long hate, and without flinch / I
bear it nobly as I live my part," says Claude McKay
in his bitterly ironic poem "The White City" (3-4).
```

[Notice that a slash [/] is used to separate lines of poetry run in with the text. The parenthetical reference cites the lines quoted.]

The List of Works Cited

Parenthetical references refer to a **Works Cited List** that includes all the sources you refer to in your paper. (If your list includes all the works consulted, whether you cite them or not, use the title *Works Consulted.*) Begin the works cited list on a new page, continuing the page numbers of the paper. For example, if the text of the paper ends on page six, the works cited section will begin on page seven.

Center the title *Works Cited* one inch from the top of the page. Arrange entries alphabetically, according to the last name of each author (or the first word of the title if the author is unknown). Articles—*a, an,* and *the*—at the beginning of a title are not considered first words. Thus, *A Handbook of Critical Approaches to Literature* would be alphabetized under *H.* In order to conserve space, publishers' names are abbreviated—for example, *Harcourt* for Harcourt Brace College Publishers. Double-space the entire works cited list between and within entries. Begin typing each entry at the left margin, and indent subsequent lines five spaces or one-half inch. The entry itself generally has three divisions—author, title, and publishing information—separated by periods.*

A book by a single author

Kingston, Maxine Hong. The Woman Warrior: Memoirs of a Girlhood among Ghosts. New York: Knopf, 1976.

A book by two or three authors

Feldman, Burton, and Robert D. Richardson. The Rise of Modern Mythology. Bloomington: Indiana UP, 1972.

[Notice that only the *first* author's name is in reverse order.]

A book by more than three authors

Guerin, Wilfred, et al., eds. A Handbook of Critical Approaches to Literature. 3rd. ed. New York: Harper, 1992.

[Instead of using *et al.,* you may list all the authors' names in the order in which they appear on the title page.]

Two or more works by the same author

Novoa, Juan-Bruce. Chicano Authors: Inquiry by Interview, Austin: U of Texas P, 1980.

---

* The fourth edition of the *MLA Handbook for Writers of Research Papers* (1995) shows a single space after all end punctuation.

> ---. "Themes in Rudolfo Anaya's Work." Address given at New Mexico State University, Las Cruces. 11 Apr. 1987.

[List two or more works by the same author in alphabetical order by title. Include the author's full name in the first entry; use three unspaced hyphens followed by a period to take the place of the author's name in second and subsequent entries.]

An edited book

> Oosthuizen, Ann, ed. <u>Sometimes When It Rains: Writings by South African Women</u>. New York: Pandora, 1987.

[Note that the abbreviation *ed.* stands for *editor.*]

A book with a volume number

> Eagleton, T. Allston. <u>A History of the New York Stage</u>. Vol. 2. Englewood Cliffs: Prentice. 1987.

[All three volumes have the same title.]

> Durant, Will, and Ariel Durant. <u>The Age of Napoleon: A History of European Civilization from 1789 to 1815</u>. New York: Simon, 1975.

[Each volume has a different title, so you may cite an individual book without referring to the other volumes.]

A short story, poem, or play in a collection of the author's work

> Gordimer, Nadine. "Once upon a Time." <u>"Jump" and Other Stories</u>. New York: Farrar, 1991. 23–30.

A short story in an anthology

> Salinas, Marta. "The Scholarship Jacket." <u>Nosotros: Latina Literature Today</u>. Ed. Maria del Carmen

Boza, Beverly Silva, and Carmen Valle. Bingham-
ton: Bilingual, 1986. 68-70.

[The inclusive page numbers follow the year of publication. Note that here
the abbreviation *Ed.* stands for *Edited by.*]

A poem in an anthology

Simmerman, Jim. "Child's Grave, Hale County, Alabama." <u>The Pushcart Prize, X: Best of the Small
Presses</u>. Ed. Bill Henderson. New York: Penguin,
1986. 198-99.

A play in an anthology

Hughes, Langston. <u>Mother and Child</u>. <u>Black Drama An-
thology</u>. Ed. Woodie King and Ron Miller. New
York: NAL, 1986.399-406.

An article in an anthology

Forster, E. M. "Flat and Round Characters." <u>The Theory of the Novel</u>. Ed. Philip Stevick. New York:
Free, 1980. 223-31.

More than one selection from the same anthology

If you are using more than one selection from an anthology, cite the anthology in one entry. In addition, list each individual selection separately, including the author and title of the selection, the anthology editor's last
name, and the inclusive page numbers.

Kirszner, Laurie G., and Stephen R. Mandell, eds.
<u>Literature: Reading, Reacting, Writing</u>. 3rd ed.
Fort Worth: Harcourt, 1997.
Rich, Adrienne. "Diving into the Wreck." Kirszner
and Mandell 874-76.

A translation

Carpentier, Alejo. <u>Reasons of State</u>. Trans. Francis
Partridge. New York: Norton, 1976.

An article in a journal with continuous pagination in each issue

```
LeGuin, Ursula K. "American Science Fiction and the
    Other." Science Fiction Studies 2 (1975):
    208-10.
```

An article with separate pagination in each issue

```
Grossman, Robert. "The Grotesque in Faulkner's
    'A Rose for Emily.'" Mosaic 20.3 (1987): 40-55.
```

[20.3 signifies volume 20, issue 3.]

An article in a magazine

```
Milosz, Czeslaw. "A Lecture." New Yorker 22 June
    1992: 32.
"Solzhenitsyn: An Artist Becomes an Exile." Time
    25 Feb. 1974: 34+.
```

[34+ indicates that the article appears on pages that are not consecutive; in this case the article begins on page 34 and then continues on page 37. An article with no listed author is entered by title on the works cited list.]

An article in a daily newspaper

```
Oates, Joyce Carol. "When Characters from the Page
    Are Made Flesh on the Screen." New York Times
    23 Mar. 1986, late ed.: C1+.
```

[C1+ indicates that the article begins on page 1 of Section C and continues on a subsequent page.]

An article in a reference book

```
"Dance Theatre of Harlem." The New Encyclopaedia
    Britannica: Micropaedia. 15th ed. 1987.
```

[You do not need to include publication information for well-known reference books.]

```
Grimstead, David. "Fuller, Margaret Sarah." Encyclo-
    pedia of American Biography. Ed. John A. Gar-
    raty. New York: Harper, 1974.
```

[You must include publication information when citing reference books that are not well known.]

A CD-ROM: Entry with a print version

> Zurbach, Kate. "The Linguistic Roots of Three
> Terms." <u>Linguistic Quarterly</u> 37 (1994): 12–47.
> <u>Infotrac: Magazine Index Plus</u>. CD-ROM. Informa-
> tion Access. Jan. 1996.

[When you cite information with a print version from a CD-ROM, include the publication information, the underlined title of the database (<u>Infotrac: Magazine Index Plus</u>), the publication medium (CD-ROM), the name of the company that produced the CD-ROM (Information Access), and the electronic publication date.]

A CD-ROM: Entry with no print version

> "Surrealism." <u>Encarta 1996</u>. CD-ROM. Redmond: Micro-
> soft, 1996.

[If you are citing a part of a work, include the title in quotation marks.]

> <u>A Music Lover's Multimedia Guide to Beethoven's 5th</u>.
> CD-ROM. Spring Valley: Interactive, 1993.

[If you are citing an entire work, include the underlined title.]

An online source: Entry with a print version

> Dekoven, Marianne. "Utopias Limited: Post-sixties
> and Postmodern American Fiction." <u>Modern
> Fiction Studies</u> 41.1 (Spring 1995): 121–34.
> 17 Mar. 1996 <http://muse.jhu.edu/journals/MFS/
> v041/41.1 dekoven.html>.

[When you cite information with a print version from an online source, include the publication information for the printed source, the number of pages or the number of paragraphs (if available), and the date of access. Include the electronic address, or URL, in angle brackets. Information from a commercial computer service—America Online, Prodigy, and CompuServ, for example—will not have an electronic address.]

> O'Hara, Sandra. "Reexamining the Canon." <u>Time</u> 13 May
> 1994: 27. America Online. 22 Aug. 1994.

An online source: Entry with no print version

> "Romanticism." <u>Academic American Encyclopedia</u>. Sept.
>   1996. Prodigy. 6 Nov. 1995.

[This entry shows that the material was accessed on November 6, 1996.]

An online source: Public Posting

> Peters, Olaf. "Studying English through German."
>   Online posting. 29 Feb. 1996. Foreign Language
>   Forum, Multi Language Section. CompuServe.
>   15 Mar. 1996.
> Gilford, Mary. "Dog Heroes in Children's Litera-
>   ture." 4 Oct. 1996. Newsgroup alt.animals.dogs.
>   America Online. 23 Mar. 1996.

[**WARNING:** Using information from online forums and newsgroups is risky. Contributors are not necessarily experts, and frequently they are incorrect and misinformed. Unless you can be certain that the information you are receiving from these sources is reliable, do not use it in your papers.]

An online source: Electronic Text

> Twain, Mark. <u>The Adventures of Huckleberry Finn</u>.
>   From <u>The Writing of Mark Twain</u>. Vol. 13.
>   New York: Harper, 1970. <u>Wiretap.spies</u>.
>   13 Jan. 1996 <http.//www.sci.dixie.edu/
>   DixieCollege/Ebooks/huckfin.html>.

[This electronic text was originally published by Harper. The name of the repository for the electronic edition is Wiretap.spies. (underlined).]

An online source: E-Mail

> Adkins, Camille. E-Mail to the author. 8 June 1995.

An interview

> Brooks, Gwendolyn. "Interviews." <u>Triquarterly</u> 60
>   (1984): 405–10.

A lecture or address

> Novoa, Juan-Bruce. "Themes in Rudolfo Anaya's Work."
>   New Mexico State University, Las Cruces,
>   11 Apr. 1987.

A film or videocassette

> "A Worn Path." By Eudora Welty. Dir. John Reid and
>   Claudia Velasco. Perf. Cora Lee Day and Con-
>   chita Ferrell. Videocassette. Harcourt, 1994.

[In addition to the title, the director, and the year, include other pertinent information such as the principal performers.]

Explanatory Notes

Explanatory notes, indicated by a superscript (a raised number) in the text, may be used to cite several sources at once or to provide commentary or explanations that do not fit smoothly into your paper. The full text of these notes appears on the first numbered page following the last page of the paper. (If your paper has no explanatory notes, the works cited page follows the last page of the paper.) Like works cited entries, explanatory notes are double-spaced within and between entries. However, the first line of each explanatory note is indented five spaces (or one-half inch), with subsequent lines flush with the left-hand margin.

TO CITE SEVERAL SOURCES

In the paper

> Surprising as it may seem, there have been many
> attempts to define literature.[1]

In the note

> [1] For an overview of critical opinion, see Arnold
> 72; Eagleton 1-2; Howe 43-44; and Abrams 232-34.

TO PROVIDE EXPLANATIONS

In the paper

In recent years gothic novels have achieved great popularity.[3]

In the note

[3] Gothic novels, works written in imitation of medieval romances, originally relied on supernatural occurrences. They flourished in the late eighteenth and early nineteenth centuries.

Credits

Herman Beavers, "Dead Rocks and Sleeping Men: Aurality in the Aesthetic of Langston Hughes" by Herman Beavers reprinted from *The Langston Hughes Review*, 11.1 (Spring 1992). Copyright by The Langston Hughes Society. Reproduced by permission.

Karen Jackson Ford, "Do Right to Write Right: Langston Hughes's Aesthetics of Simplicity" by Karen Jackson Ford originally printed in *Twentieth Century Literature* (Vol. 38, No. 4—Winter 1992, pp. 436–56).

Langston Hughes, "The Negro Artist and the Racial Mountain" by Langston Hughes. Reprinted with permission from the June 23, 1926 issue of *The Nation*. Copyright 1926.

———. "To Negro Writers." Reprinted by permission of Harold Ober Associates Incorporated. Copyright 1935 by Langston Hughes.

———. "My Adventures as a Social Poet." Reprinted by permission of Harold Ober Associates Incorporated. Copyright 1947 by Langston Hughes.

———. "Langston Hughes Speaks" by Langston Hughes as it appeared in *The Crisis*, May 1953. The author wishes to thank The Crisis Publishing Co., Inc., the magazine of the National Association for the Advancement of Colored People, for authorizing the use of this work.

———. "Swinging High" from *Simple's Uncle Sam* by Langston Hughes, compilation by Arnold Rampersad and Ramona Bass. Copyright © 1993 by Arnold Rampersad and Ramona Bass. Reprinted by permission of Hill and Wang, a division of Farrar, Straus & Giroux, Inc.

———. "The Negro Speaks of Rivers," "The Weary Blues," "I, Too," "Let America Be America Again," "Ballad of the Landlord," "Theme for English B," "Dream Boogie," "Dream Deferred," and "Birmingham Sunday" from *Collected Poems* by Langston Hughes. Copyright © 1994 by the Estate of Langston Hughes. Reprinted by permission of Alfred A. Knopf, Inc.

Robert K. Martin, "Langston Hughes and the 'Other' Whitman" reprinted from *The Continuing Presence of Walt Whitman: The Life after the Life*, edited by Robert K. Martin by permission of the University of Iowa Press. Copyright © 1992 by University of Iowa Press.